THE LIFE OF SAINT NICHOLAS OF SION

Frontispiece: Icon of St. Nicholas with scenes from his Life. Mount Sinai, St. Catherine's Monastery. Late twelfth century.

The Archbishop Iakovos Library of
Ecclesiastical and Historical Sources No. 10

N.M. Vaporis, General Editor

THE LIFE OF SAINT NICHOLAS OF SION

Text and Translation

by

IHOR ŠEVČENKO

and

NANCY PATTERSON ŠEVČENKO

HELLENIC COLLEGE PRESS

The Life of

SAINT NICHOLAS OF SION

Text and Translation

by

IHOR ŠEVČENKO

and

NANCY PATTERSON ŠEVČENKO

HELLENIC COLLEGE PRESS
Brookline, Massachusetts 02146

Financial assistance toward the publication of this book was provided by the Taylor Foundation.

Published by HELLENIC COLLEGE PRESS
50 Goddard Avenue
Brookline, Massachussetts 02146

Cover design by MARY C. VAPORIS

Library of Congress Cataloging in Publication Data
Vios kai politeia tou en hagiois patros hemôn Nikolaou
    archimandritou genamenou tês hagias Siôn kai
    Episkopou tês Pinareôn poleôs. English and Greek.
The Life of Saint Nicholas of Sion.

(The Archbishop Iakovos library of ecclesiastical and
historical sources; no.10)
    Bibliography: p.
    Includes indexes
    1. Nicholas, of Sion, Saint, d. 564. 2. Christian saints—
Turkey—Biography. I. Ševčenko, Ihor. II. Ševčenko, Nancy
Patterson. III. Title. IV. Series.
BR1720.N48V56 1984   270.2'092'4 [B]   84-27966
ISBN 0-917653-02-5
ISBN 0-917653-03-3 (pbk.)

CONTENTS

LIST OF ILLUSTRATIONS

Dust jacket and paperbound front cover: Sea scene with devils, detail. Staro Nagoričane. Church of St. George. Early fourteenth century.

Dust jacket, and paperbound back cover: Book cover in silver with gilding from Holy Sion Monastery. Found at Kumluca, now at Dumbarton Oaks. Mid sixth century.

Half-title page, Text and Translation page, Plates page, and Indices page: Roundel with inscription "Holy Sion, help." Detail of an oblong polykandelon in silver from Holy Sion Monastery. Found at Kumluca, now at Dumbarton Oaks. Mid sixth century.

Frontispiece: Icon of St. Nicholas of Myra with scenes from his Life. Mount Sinai, St. Catherine's Monastery. Late twelfth century.

1. The Birth of St. Nicholas. Detail from an icon of St. Nicholas, Mount Sinai, St. Catherine's Monastery. Late twelfth century.

2. The Schooling of St. Nicholas. Detail from an icon of St. Nicholas, Patmos, Monastery of St. John the Theologian. Fifteenth century.

3. St. Nicholas fells the cypress of Plakoma. Agoriane, Church of St. Nicholas. Late thirteenth century.

4. St. Nicholas fells the cypress of Plakoma. Staro Nagoričane, Church of St. George. Early fourteenth century.

5. Sea scene with devils. Staro Nagoričane, Church of St. George. Early fourteenth century.

6. Sea scene with devils and Ammonios. Platsa, Church of St. Nicholas of Kampinari. Mid fourteenth century.

7. Sea scene Sucevița, Church of the Resurrection. Ca. 1600.

8. St. Nicholas heals the demoniac brought to the vineyard. Sucevița, Church of the Resurrection. Ca. 1600.

9. St. Nicholas is consecrated bishop. Sucevița, Church of the Resurrection. Ca. 1600.

10. The Death of St. Nicholas. Meteora, Church of St. Nicholas Anapausas. First half of the sixteenth century.

11. The Death of St. Nicholas, detail: singers. Markov Manastir, Church of St. Demetrios. Second half of the fourteenth century.

12. The Death of St. Nicholas. Sucevița, Church of the Resurrection. Ca. 1600.

13. Oblong polykandelon in silver from Holy Sion Monastery. Found at Kumluca, now at Dumbarton Oaks. Mid sixth century.

14. Large silver paten with engraved cross from Holy Sion Monastery. Found at Kumluca, now at Dumbarton Oaks. Mid sixth century.
15. Cruciform polykandelon in silver from Holy Sion Monastery. Found at Kumluca, now at Dumbarton Oaks. Mid sixth century.
16. Openwork silver container for an oil lamp from Holy Sion Monastery. Found at Kumluca, now at Dumbarton Oaks. Mid sixth century.

PHOTO CREDITS

Frontispiece, Fig, 1: Reproduced through the courtesy of the Michigan-Princeton-Alexandria Expedition to Mount Sinai
Fig. 2: S. Papadopoulos, Athens
Fig. 3: E. Konstantinides, Athens
Dust jacket (front), Figs. 4, 5, 11: Ihor Ševčenko, Cambridge, Mass
Fig. 6: Doula Mouriki and Rena Andreades, Athens
Figs. 7-9, 12: Cyril Mango, Oxford
Fig. 10: M. Chatzidakis, Athens
Dust jacket (back), title page, Figs. 13-16: Dumbarton Oaks Center for Byzantine Studies, Washington, D.C.

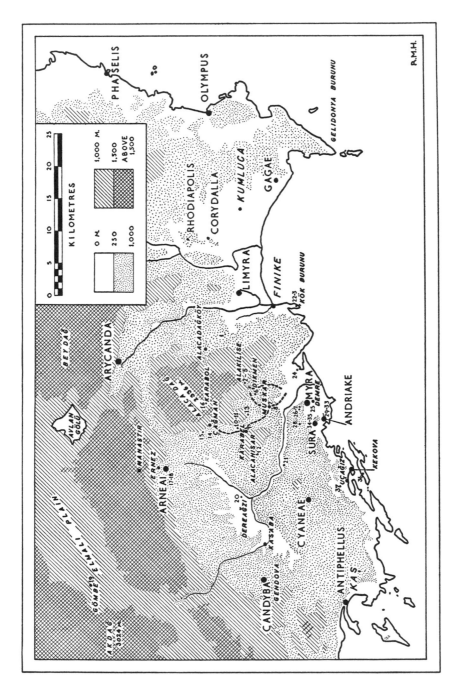

Map of central and south-eastern Lycia. Ancient roads are shown by broken lines.
[After R. M. Harrison]

Introduction

Lycia, a mountainous coastal region of southwestern Asia Minor, is best known to Christians east and west as the place of the early cult of Saint Nicholas. The center of the cult was in Myra (today's Demre or Kale), the capital city of Lycia and the presumed episcopal see of the Saint Nicholas of Myra, who according to tradition had been a contemporary of the Emperor Constantine the Great (d. 337). Nicholas was still a somewhat shadowy figure as late as the mid-sixth century; but as time went on, he became one of the most popular saints of all Christendom and was ultimately transformed in the West into our Santa Claus.

In the present little book we are offering the text and translation of the Life of another saint named Nicholas. This other Nicholas flourished in the first half of the sixth century and, like Nicholas of Myra, was active in Lycia: he was abbot of the Monastery of Holy Sion near Myra and was subsequently ordained bishop of Pinara in western Lycia. Unlike Nicholas bishop of Myra, about whom we have little reliable information, Nicholas of Sion was an historical figure of flesh and blood.

The historical value of the Life of Nicholas of Sion is enhanced by the fact that it was written soon after the Saint's death, which can be dated with a great degree of probability to the year 564. The author of our Life must have been a person of the Saint's entourage and may have even been one of the attendants who accompanied Nicholas in his travels. The latter conjecture is suggested by the use of the first person plural in the chapters describing the Saint's journeys to the Holy Land (**9; 27; 28; 32**).[1] In any case, the author was intimately familiar with the Sion Monastery; he may even have been one of those who attended the Saint's last moments on earth. If that is true, our candidates for the author of the Life are ''Nicholas the deacon and cellarer,'' ''Paul [son] of Hermaios, the most devout deacon from the hamlet of Oumbe,'' ''Nicholas, most devout archdeacon,'' or, conceivably, our Nicholas' own brother, Hermaios (cf. **78-79**).

---

[1]Numbers in bold face refer to chapters in the Life of Saint Nicholas of Sion.

We assume that the author of our Life drew largely upon his or his informants' personal recollections. In addition to these, he may have relied on some written reports, such as the records of the Sion Monastery. This is especially likely in the account of Nicholas' tours of the countryside after the bubonic plague, when the Saint had a large number of oxen slaughtered to feed a multitude of countryfolk and clerics: the figures and itineraries given in that account are so precise that they must go back to lists of itemized expenses kept at the monastery. It is also likely that the names, places of origin, and ailments of people seeking miraculous cures at the monastery were recorded, and that these records were used in our Life. The bulk of our author's sources, however, must have been oral, going as far back as two generations (cf. **10**). Even his demonology seems to use motifs circulating by word of mouth in monastic communities of the time.

Our author is unaffected by literary conventions and we do not have to go far to find his literary models: they are the New Testament and the Psalter, even though we can detect in our Life echoes of Old Testament readings and of liturgical prayers. Our author's dependence on the New Testament goes beyond obvious thematic borrowings, such as the patterning of the miraculous feeding of clerics and master craftsmen by Nicholas (**25**; **45**) on the stories of the loaves and fishes that fed the five and the four thousand (cf., e.g., Mt 15.32-39 and Mk 8.1-10); endowing the story of the storm at sea (**30**) with traits of an analogous miracle on the Sea of Galilee (cf. Mt 8.23-27; Mk 4.35-39; Lk 8.22-24); the modeling of parallels between the harvest and the plague that was to precede the end of the world (**47-52**, cf. especially **51**) on eschatological passages from the Gospels (Mt 13.30; Mk 4.29) and from the Revelation (14.15-19); or, finally, the borrowing of details in the description of Nicholas' final hour on earth (**78**) from the story of our Lord's last moments on the cross (cf. Jn 19.30; Mt 8.20; 27.50; Lk 9.58). In one case at least, our author borrows the structure of his episode from a narrative in the Scriptures, while the contents of the two remain different: the story in which the young sailor Ammonios falls from the mast and is resurrected by Nicholas (**31**) follows the pattern of the story in the Acts of the Apostles (20.9) where the youth Eutychos falls from the third floor of a house and is resurrected by Saint Paul.

Incidentally, while the fall of Eutychos is attributed to a natural cause, deep sleep, that of Ammonios is the work of the Devil.

Our Life's dependence on scriptural words and phrases is so vast as to be unparalleled in any work of hagiography known to us. It strengthens our suspicion that the Scriptures were the only literary text to which our author had been thoroughly exposed, for when we discount literal borrowings from the Scriptures, we find that our author's language is untutored. He employs half a dozen otherwise unattested words; he uses λέγοντα for λέγον, ἰδόντα for ἰδόν, δώσαντα for δόντα, and ἐλθῶτα for ἐλθόντα; he thinks that the aorist of περισσεύει is περιέσσευσεν; he combines πνεῦμα, a neuter noun, with ἐπιδεικνύων, a masculine participle; he construes ἔχειν with an infinitive to denote the future tense; and he writes ἐπῆρεν to mean "he took." In a word, there is precious little "literature" in our Life and because of this, it is as reliable a source of information as any hagiographical document contemporary with its hero can be.

The Life of Nicholas of Sion does speak of a certain "forefather" saint, also named Nicholas, of that "glorious" saint's martyrium—or "witness church"—in or near Myra and of his chapel in the nearby Kastellon (**76; 8; 57**). While these passages attest that by the end of the sixth century a Saint Nicholas had had a cult in Myra and in its neighborhood for a long time, they also clearly show that the hero of our Life was someone quite distinct from that saint. Later Byzantine hagiographers, however, blurred that distinction by borrowing many episodes of our Life and transferring them to the life of that earlier Nicholas, believed to have been bishop of Myra.

Thus the Life of Nicholas of Sion contributed to the growth of the legend of Saint Nicholas of Myra, a legend that did not take full shape in the East until the tenth century. Among the episodes that the developed versions of the legend of Saint Nicholas of Myra borrowed from our Life are, to name a few prominent stories, the miraculous events at the saint's birth (**2**); the felling of the cypress tree inhabited by a demon (**15-19**); miracles at sea (**28-32**); and the healing of the demoniac brought to the vineyard (**63**).

Having absorbed many motifs of the Life of the historical Saint Nicholas of Sion, the developed legend of Saint Nicholas of Myra overshadowed—almost supplanted—that original Life. As a result, only a few Greek manuscripts of the Life of Nicholas of Sion have been preserved, and only one of them is complete; and even in these manuscripts scribes, by then familiar with the legend of Saint Nicholas of Myra, would introduce a great deal of confusion by making, for instance, our Nicholas into a bishop of Myra instead of Pinara. Our Life fared better with the Slavs who translated a version of it relatively early; but even they assigned our Nicholas to the time of Constantine the Great—the putative period of Nicholas of Myra—rather than to the time of Justinian I under whom the historical Nicholas of Sion lived.

Thus while the historian of the cult of Saint Nicholas of Myra sees in our Life one of the preliminary stages in the formation of the full-fledged legend of that Saint, the historian of early Byzantium and the general student of hagiography values it as a source both for the facts and mental attitudes of its own time—about which we know a great deal—and for the economy, popular religiosity and above all topography of the Lycian region in the sixth century.—about which we know very little outside of our text. We are able to locate several of the sites mentioned in our Life on the modern map of Turkey: Myra itself, Phoinix (today's Finike), Arneai (today's Ernez); but neither historians nor archaeologists have been able to localize the Monastery of Holy Sion with certainty, although sites like Karabel or Manastir have been proposed. All we know for sure is that the monastery stood not far from Arneai-Ernez (cf. 39) and Phoinix-Finike (cf. 37), and that it was situated somewhere in the mountain range (cf. 38; 75) to the north of the city of Myra; yet this monastery must have been an important center of the area. For all these difficulties, our Life is a mine of potential information for a historical geographer: it contains dozens of place names, most of them non-Greek sounding, such as Karkabo and Oualo (although names such as Nea Kome [56; 57] Symbolon [57] or Zenoupolis [40], presumably a recent foundation, do occasionally occur), and of shrines; we can often puzzle out how these sites were related to one another, but are not yet able to pin down their absolute location. The historian of antique religion searches our Life for the traces of paganism (such as the communal banquets and the cult of sacred trees) surviving two and a half centuries after the official adoption of Christianity throughout the Empire.

You do not have to be a professional scholar to appreciate the Life of Saint Nicholas of Sion. A mere friend of the past and an enlightened believer will be captivated by its closeness to the events it describes; by its down-to-earth piety—Nicholas's cures sometimes resemble work-therapy (cf. **63**), and often take quite some time, thirty or forty days, to produce results (cf. **61; 65; 66; 74**); and his expectation of the end of the world (**48; 51**) is within the range of what must have been considered the realm of reality in the sixth-century Lycian mountains—; and by its overall simplicity.

Overall simplicity, however, does not mean that our Life is free of complications. Sometimes we are at a loss to explain these complications: they may be unintentional and due to an author who lacks the skill needed for integrating his material; or a purpose may be hiding beneath them. The flashback (**39**), after the story of the second journey to the Holy Land, to the time of the first journey and of the building of the monastery (**7-8**) may be a case of helplessness; furthermore, on four occasions (**21; 23; 24; 53**) our author forgets to finish his story. But take the chapters at the beginning that deal with the early history of the monastery: there, doublets appear, telling a similar story twice (compare **4-7** with **10-14**). Are they due to the awkward conflation of two traditions, or do they serve to obscure the fact that the Saint's uncle, rather than the Saint himself, was the true founder of the monastery? And were there two voyages to the Holy Land by Nicholas of Sion, as the Life explicitly states (**27**), or one by his uncle, another by himself (compare **8-9** with **27-38**)?

In other cases, however, there is little doubt that our author controls the narrative rather than being led by it. He does it when he reveals the tensions between the Saint's elder brother and successor, Artemas, and the Saint himself, tensions that may be the author's own (cf. **39**, where Artemas usurps powers that Nicholas has reserved for himself; **44**, where he resents having to work while his brother rests; **47**, where he begrudges his brother's proposal to offer three loaves to an angel [all this in Nicholas' dream!]; and **48**, where he gives no credence to Nicholas' prophetic vision). The author also glosses over, without concealing them, the difficulties that Nicholas encountered in his bishopric at Pinara (three years after his ordination, he quarreled with the local magistrates and clergy over the site of the shrine of Virgin Mary; it seems that as a result, he had to return to his monastery, keeping, of course, his episcopal title: cf. **69; 72; 80**); and we are not told why our Nicholas was buried by Philip, bishop of Phellos **(79)** rather than by the archbishop of nearby Myra, although we do hear of accusations the archbishop of Myra leveled against Nicholas some twenty years before the latter's death (before the plague, Nicholas appointed himself through a vision as the "harvester-saint," to receive and pray for the souls of the dead from Lycia; during the plague, he was accused of endangering the food supply of the city [cf. **47-53**]). Finally, our author knows his titulature quite well: he combines the superlative "most beloved of God" (θεοφιλέστατος; in the sixth century, a standard epithet for a bishop), with the name of our Nicholas only after he has elevated him to the episcopal throne (cf. **72; 73; 75;** and **68** respectively).

The general reader will not have to pay much attention to these finer points to enjoy our Life. It will be enough for him to keep a few facts and dates in mind during his reading: that Nicholas passed the better part of his life under the Byzantine emperor Justinian I (527-565); that the bubonic plague which affected the whole East began in 541/2; that the Monastery of Holy Sion, provincial as it was, was quite large (at one point, eighty-three workers took part in the construction of its shrine, cf. **45**); that it was also very rich, as can be deduced both from the high cost of Nicholas' banqueting tours of the countryside (cf. **54-57**) and from the luxurious vessels, patens and candelabra dedicated to it and discovered at Kumluca (east of Finike) in the early 1960s (cf. figs. 13-16 below; at present, these treasures are divided between the museums of Dumbarton Oaks in Washington, D.C., and Antalya in Turkey, some 70 miles northeast of Myra); that Nicholas was rich as bishop of Pinara as well, for he could afford spending four hundred gold pieces for a shrine of the Virgin Mary there **(69)**; that he was quite powerful, for as abbot of Holy Sion, assured of the support of his Lycian mountaineers, he was apparently able to defy the orders for his arrest, issued both by the archbishop and by the governor of Myra (**53**); that, although we hear of clergy in the countryside and although paganism is never directly mentioned in the Life (except perhaps for the episode of the felling of the cypress tree, still called "holy tree" in **15-16** and **18-20**), the Saint's miracles and banquets that he gave on the two occasions when he toured the countryside seem to be a part of missionary propaganda among imperfectly—or not at all—Christianized mountain folk (**54-57**); and that both Nicholas and his monastery stood in a close relationship to Jerusalem. This close relationship explains the monastery's name of Holy Sion; it is also the reason for our putting the death of our Life's hero in the years of Makarios II, the Patriarch of Jerusalem (second patriarchate: 563/4-ca. 575).

Along with our translation, we reproduce the Greek text of the Life, in view of its great rarity in this country. Basically, we have adopted the edition made by Gustav Anrich in 1913, even though we were aware that on occasion his text is arbitrary or in need of emendation (cf., e.g., **78** for a likely confusion in the names of those present at Nicholas' deathbed or the loss of the name of Nicholas' brother Hermaios). Anrich mainly relied on the *Vaticanus Graecus* 821, of the eleventh century (and should have followed it even more closely). We depart from Anrich in one sizable section and in two short passages (**5-8, 31, 39**), and in over ninety individual readings. Almost all our changes and corrections come from the *Vaticanus* and the *Sinaiticus Graecus* 525, probably of the eleventh century; this manuscript is interpolated and contains miracles of later date, but can be used to improve upon the readings of the *Vaticanus*. The *Sinaiticus* was known to Anrich, but was inaccessible to him. Thus he retranslated its relevant passages into Greek from a modern Russian translation; we reproduce the original. For the scholars' convenience, the passages from the *Sinaiticus* and all our other departures from Anrich's text (except for punctuation) are set in Greek italics. We also give the page numbers of the Anrich edition in the margins of our Greek text.

In our translation we have decided to remain close to the simplicity and occasional helplessness of the original. In rendering the many words or phrases borrowed from the New Testament and the Psalter we usually rely on the King James Version. Thus in the very first line of the Life, ἀνακεφαλαιοῦσθαι is translated by "to gather together in one" (cf. Ephesians 1.10). All added material in our translation is enclosed in square (rather than pointed) brackets; passages that remain still unclear to us are provided with a question mark. We did not try to standardize the terminology and the clichés of the Life except for the three territorial terms χώρα, κώμη and χωρίον. We rendered them by district, village and hamlet respectively, although we were aware that the same locality may be called both district and village (so Traglassos, cf.1; 9; 53).

Our Life cries for a commentary. An attempt to provide one here would go beyond the purpose of this small book, which is to put a highly valuable but relatively inaccessible early Byzantine hagiographical text into the hands of both the professional and the general reader. To help the latter, twenty terms have been alphabetically arranged and explained (cf. pp. 135-40). For the benefit of both the scholar and the general reader, we compiled a list of Scriptural quotations and allusions occurring in our Life (cf. pp. 141-49). This list, though surely incomplete, goes well beyond the information contained in Anrich's apparatus.

Finally, a word about illustrations. Five of them (figs. 7-9; 12-13) appear here for the first time. We reproduced only such pictorial narrative material of the legend of Saint Nicholas of Myra that goes back to the Life of Nicholas of Sion. It comes from Mount Sinai in Egypt; from Meteora, Agoriane, Platsa and Patmos in Greece; from Staro Nagoričane and Markov Manastir in Yugoslav Macedonia; and from Suceviţa in Moldavia (today's northern Roumania). It ranges in date from the twelfth century to about the year 1600. This wide spread in space and time should give an idea of the wide extent of the cult of Saint Nicholas in the Byzantine and post-Byzantine worlds, an area where unity of culture transcended boundaries of state, language and chronology. We also included illustrations of some representative examples of the Dumbarton Oaks part of the Kumluca treasure, various pieces of which can in our view be safely connected with the Holy Sion Monastery.

For a fuller pictorial documentation and bibliography the reader may consult Nancy P. Ševčenko, *The Life of Saint Nicholas in Byzantine Art* (Turin, 1983). For all the early texts connected with the cult of Saint Nicholas of Myra and for the story of the growth of this cult in the East we refer the reader to the fundamental work by Gustav Anrich, *Der heilige Nikolaos in der griechischen Kirche. Texte und Untersuchungen,* I (Die Texte); II (Prolegomena, Untersuchungen, Indices) (Leipzig-Berlin, 1913-1917). The growth of the cult of Saint Nicholas in the West has been well researched by Karl Meisen, *Nikolauskult und Nikolausbrauch im Abendlande* (Düsseldorf, 1931). For a popular, but well-informed overall treatment of the Nicholas legend (with a few pages devoted to our Life), cf. Charles W. Jones, *Saint Nicholas of Myra, Bari and Manhattan. Biography of a Legend* (Chicago, 1978) and Rüdiger Müller, *Sankt Nikolaus, der Heilige der Ost- und Westkirche* (Freiburg i. Br., 1982). For a treatment of the historical geography and the survival of pagan cults reflected in the Life, the most useful article to date is that by Louis Robert, "Villes et monnaies de Lycie," *Hellenica*, 10 (1955), 188-222. For the proposal to localize the Monastery of Holy Sion at Karabel, north-west of Myra, cf. R. Martin Harrison, "Churches and Chapels in Central Lycia," *Anatolian Studies,* 13 (1963), 117-51, esp. 131-35, 150; cf. also H. G. Severin, "Byzantinische Provinz," *Berliner Museen* (October, 1977), 10-12.

Our map of the area of Sion is borrowed from Harrison's article, p. 123 (we added two place-names: Manastir and Kumluca). We thank the Michigan-Princeton-Alexandria Expedition, the Dumbarton Oaks Center for Byzantine Studies, Miss Susan Boyd, Professor M. Chatzidakis, Mrs. E. Konstantinides, Professors Cyril Mango and Doula Mouriki, Mrs. Rena Andreades, and Mr. S. Papadopoulos for providing us with photographs or helping us to obtain them. We are grateful to Dr. Angela Hero for help in proofreading and for several suggestions concerning the translation.

Our warmest thanks go to Father Nomikos Vaporis for including our book in the Archbishop Iakovos Library series under his editorship, and for preparing the draft of the General Index.

TEXT AND TRANSLATION

3A **Βίος καὶ πολιτεία τοῦ ἐν ἁγίοις πατρὸς ἡμῶν Νικο-λάου ἀρχιμανδρίτου γεναμένου ⟨ τῆς ἁγίας Σιὼν καὶ ἐπισκόπου τῆς Πιναρέων πόλεως ⟩.**

1. Ἐν ταῖς ἡμέραις ἐκείναις ηὐδόκησεν ὁ θεὸς ἀνα-κεφαλαιοῦσθαι τὰς γραφὰς τὰς διὰ τῶν προφη-τῶν κηρυχθείσας εἰς τὸν κύριον ἡμῶν Ἰησοῦν Χριστόν. αἱ γὰρ τῶν ἁγίων προφητῶν ῥήσεις προδηλοῦσιν καὶ τὰς
5 τῶν δικαίων ἁγίας κλήσεις καὶ ὀνομασίας τὰς λεγούσας· «δεῦτε, οἱ εὐλογημένοι τοῦ πατρός μου, κληρονομήσατε τὴν ἡτοιμασμένην ὑμῖν βασιλείαν» ἐν τοῖς οὐρανοῖς. βου-λήσει γὰρ τοῦ ἀγαθοῦ θεοῦ ἐγένετό τις ἀνὴρ θαυμαστὸς καὶ ὅσιος παρὰ θεῷ, ὀνόματι Νικόλαος, ἐν χώρᾳ Τρα-
10 γλασσῶν, ἐν χωρίῳ Φαρρῶα· οὗτος ⟨ ἦν ⟩ ἐκλελεγμένος καὶ εὐάρεστος τῷ θεῷ. καὶ οὗτος ηὐδόκησεν συνοικῆσαι σὺν τῷ πνευματικῷ πατρὶ καὶ ἀρχιμανδρίτῃ Σαββατίῳ. καὶ ὄντων αὐτῶν ἐν τῇ ἁγίᾳ καὶ ἐνδόξῳ μονῇ τῶν Ἀκα-λισσέων, κατὰ ἐμφάνισιν τῶν πάντων κτίστου καὶ
15 δεσπότου Χριστοῦ ἐβουλεύσατο τῇ τοῦ θεοῦ βουλήσει εἰς μνημόσυνον καὶ ἱλαστήριον ἁμαρτιῶν κτίζειν τὸν ἔν-δοξον καὶ ἀσάλευτον οἶκον τῆς ἐνδόξου ἁγίας Σιών.

The Life and Conduct of our Father Nicholas, Dwelling Among the Saints, the Late Archimandrite [of Holy Sion, and Bishop of the City of Pinara].

1. In those days it pleased God to gather together in one what the Scriptures had proclaimed through the Prophets concerning our Lord Jesus Christ. For the sayings of the holy Prophets also foreshadow the holy summons and designations of the righteous, which run: "Come, ye blessed of my Father, inherit the Kingdom prepared for you" in Heaven. For by the will of the good Lord, in the district of the Traglassians, in the hamlet of Pharroa, there was a wondrous man, holy before God, whose name was Nicholas. He was the elect of the Lord, Who was well-pleased with him. And it pleased Nicholas to dwell together with his spiritual father and archimandrite Sabbatios; and while they were dwelling in the holy and glorious Monastery of Akalissos, Nicholas decided to found, according to God's wish, [and] through a revelation [that came from] Christ the Founder and the Lord of all things, the glorious and enduring shrine of glorious Holy Sion, as a memorial and for the propitiation of his sins.

4Α **2.** Καὶ τοῦ τοιούτου σφραγίσματος γενομένου, ηὐδόκησεν ὁ δεσπότης τῶν ὅλων κυοφορεῖσθαι ἐν τῷ τῆς σφρα-
γίσεως τῆς ἐνδόξου ἁγίας Σιὼν παρακειμένῳ ἀγρῷ παιδίον εὐπρεπές, ἀστεῖον τῷ θεῷ, ἐκ γένους τοῦ προλεχ-
5 θέντος ὁσίου ἀνδρὸς Νικολάου, ἐκ πατρὸς μὲν Ἐπιφανίου, μητρὸς δὲ Νόννας. καὶ ἰδόντες τὸ παιδίον λίαν εὐά-
ρεστον τῷ θεῷ καὶ ἀστεῖον γεννηθέντα, ἐπωνόμασαν τὸ
ὄνομα αὐτοῦ Νικόλαον. ἅμα γὰρ τῷ κυηθῆναι αὐτόν,
ὄντα ἔτι ἐν τῇ σκάφῃ, τῇ τοῦ θεοῦ δυνάμει ἔστη ἐπὶ τοὺς
10 πόδας αὐτοῦ ὀρθὸς ὡς ὥρας δύο. καὶ ἔμφοβοι γενάμενοι
οἱ γονεῖς αὐτοῦ ἐδόξασαν τὸν θεόν. καὶ ἀπελθόντες ἐν
τῇ μονῇ τῶν Ἀκαλισσέων πρὸς τὸν ὅσιον ἄνδρα Νικόλαον, τὸν θεῖον τοῦ παιδίου, εἶπον αὐτῷ τὰ τῆς κυήσεως
τοῦ παιδίου καὶ πῶς ὀρθὸς ἔστη ἐν τῇ σκάφῃ μέχρι δύο
15 ὡρῶν. καὶ προσευξάμενος εἶπεν· 'Δόξα σοι, ὁ θεός, ὅτι
ἐγεννήθη ἡμῖν ἄνθρωπος δοῦλος τοῦ θεοῦ·' καὶ παρήγ-
γειλεν αὐτοῖς, μηδενὶ εἰπεῖν τοῦτο. 'Οὗτος γὰρ θελήματι θεοῦ ἐγεννήθη, ὃς δοξάσει τὸν θεὸν ἐν τῷ τόπῳ τούτῳ.'

3. Καὶ γεναμένου τοῦ παιδὸς ἑπταετοῦς, ἐβουλεύσαντο
τῇ τοῦ θεοῦ βουλήσει παραδοῦναι αὐτὸν εἰς μάθησιν τῶν
γραμμάτων. τοῦ γὰρ ἁγίου πνεύματος ὑπουργοῦντος καὶ
ἀπείρου ὄντος τοῦ τότε αὐτοῦ διδασκάλου, τὸ παιδίον
5 Νικόλαος τῷ ἑαυτοῦ διδασκάλῳ ὀνόματα ἐσήμαινεν,
5Α τὴν τοῦ ἁγίου πνεύματος ἔχων χάριν, ἐπὶ τῷ ἑκάστῳ
συλλαβίῳ γράφειν αὐτῷ· πορευομένου δὲ αὐτοῦ πρὸς
τὴν τῶν γραμμάτων μάθησιν, ἀπαντᾷ αὐτῷ γυνὴ ἀπὸ
τῆς κώμης, ὀνόματι Νοννίνη, ἔχουσα ξηρὸν τὸν πόδα.
10 καὶ σφραγίσας αὐτὴν τῷ σημείῳ τοῦ σταυροῦ, τῇ δυνάμει τοῦ ἁγίου πνεύματος ἐπορεύθη ὑγιής, δοξάζουσα τὸν
κύριον ἡμῶν Ἰησοῦν Χριστόν.

2. And when [the site of such] a [shrine] had been consecrated, it pleased the Lord of all that a fine child, goodly in the eyes of God, was conceived on the piece of property neighboring that which had been consecrated for glorious Holy Sion. He was related to the aforementioned holy man Nicholas, his father being Epiphanios and his mother Nonna. And when they saw that the newborn child was very pleasing to God and goodly, they called his name Nicholas. For at the time of his birth while he was still in the washbasin, by the power of God he stood upright on his feet for about two hours. And awestruck, his parents praised God. And they went to the Monastery of Akalissos, to the holy man Nicholas, the uncle of the child, and told him about the birth of the child, and how he stood upright in the basin for as much as two hours. And when the uncle had offered prayers, he said " Glory be to Thee, O God, for a servant of God has been born to us." And he enjoined them to speak of it to no one. "For he was born by the will of God and he shall glorify God in this [very] place."

3. And when the child was seven years old, they resolved, in accordance with God's will, to hand him over to learn his letters. Assisted by the Holy Spirit (his teacher of that time being inexperienced), the child Nicholas indicated [?] the words to his own teacher, by the grace of the Holy Spirit, so that he would write [these words] for him syllable by syllable [?]. And once, when he was on his way to his lessons, a woman from the village came up to him, Nonnine by name, who had a withered foot. And he made the sign of the cross over her, and by the power of the Holy Spirit she walked away made whole, glorifying our Lord Jesus Christ.

4. Ἰδὼν δὲ ὁ ὅσιος Νικόλαος, ὁ τούτου θεῖος, τὸν ἀγῶνα καὶ τὴν σπουδὴν τοῦ παιδίου, ἣν εἶχεν πρὸς τὸν τῶν
πάντων κτίστην θεόν, παρακλήσεις ἐσήμανεν τῷ ὁσιω-
τάτῳ καὶ μακαριωτάτῳ ἀρχιεπισκόπῳ Νικολάῳ, ἐπὶ τῷ
5 σφραγίσαι ἐν Φαρρώοις εὐκτήριον οἶκον. παρακληθεὶς
οὖν ὁ προλεχθεὶς ὁσιώτατος ἀρχιεπίσκοπος ἐπέδωκεν
τοῦ σφραγισθῆναι ἐν τῷ τόπῳ ἐκείνῳ εὐκτήριον, ὅ, ἐὰν
βούληται, ἐπονομάσαι ὁ ὁσιώτατος ἀρχιμανδρίτης Νι-
10 κόλαος. καὶ ἐπιστὰς τῷ τόπῳ ἐπωνόμασεν τὸ κτίσμα
τῆς ἁγίας καὶ ἐνδόξου Σιών, ἐπαρξάμενος τῇ τῶν κογ-
χῶν περιχαραγῇ. καθὼς τὸ πνεῦμα τὸ ἅγιον ἐν ταῖς Γενε-
αλογίαις λέγει· «ἐν ἀρχῇ ἐποίησεν ὁ θεὸς τὸν οὐρανόν,»
καὶ μετὰ τὸν οὐρανὸν τὸ ἔδαφος, «τὴν γῆν, ἐθεμελίω-
6Α 15 σεν,» οὕτως οὖν καὶ ἐν τῷ κτίσματι τῆς ἐνδόξου ἁγίας
Σιὼν τὸ πνεῦμα τὸ ἅγιον ἐμήνυσεν.

5. Ἅμα γὰρ τῷ αὐξάνεσθαι τὸ παιδίον Νικόλαος διὰ
τοῦ πνεύματος, θεοῦ χάριτι καὶ ὁ ναὸς ἐτελειοῦτο. συνέ-
ζευξεν δὲ αὐτῷ ὁ ὁσιώτατος αὐτοῦ θεῖος καὶ ἀρχιμανδρίτης Νικόλαος τὸν πρεσβύτερον Κόνωνα, τὸν ἐπιστά-
5 την τοῦ κτίσματος τοῦ ναοῦ τῆς ἁγίας Σιών, καὶ ἀπήγα-
γεν αὐτὸν πρὸς τὸν μακάριον καὶ ὁσιώτατον ἀρχιεπί-
σκοπον Νικόλαον ἐπὶ τὸ χειροτονῆσαι αὐτὸν ἀναγνώστην. ἰδὼν δὲ ὁ ὁσιώτατος ἀρχιεπίσκοπος *τὸν χαρακτῆρα*
τοῦ παιδίου πλήρη [πλήρις ms] *χάριτος ὄντα, ἐπέγνω τῷ*
10 *πνεύματι ὅτι μέλλει «σκεῦος ἐκλογῆς» γενέσθαι τοῦ*
κυρίου· καὶ λαβὼν καὶ εὐλογήσας, ἐχειροτόνησεν αὐτὸν
τῇ τάξει τῶν ἀναγνωστῶν, μὴ λαβὼν παρ' αὐτοῦ χειρο-
τονίας ἕνεκεν τὸ σύνολον.

4. When the holy Nicholas, his uncle, saw the strivings and earnestness of the child with respect to God the Founder of all things, he directed a request to the most holy and blessed Archbishop Nicholas that he consecrate the site of a shrine in Pharroa. At this request, the aforementioned most holy archbishop agreed to consecrate the site of a shrine in that place, which shrine the most holy Archimandrite Nicholas could name as he wished. And arriving at the place, he gave the foundation the name of Holy and glorious Sion, and he began by tracing the outlines of the apses. Just as the Holy Spirit says in Genesis: "In the beginning God created the heaven" and after the heaven, He laid the ground, that is, "the foundation of the earth," so also in the foundation of glorious Holy Sion did the Holy Spirit speak forth.

5. While the child Nicholas was growing up, guided by the [Holy] Spirit, the church was being completed by the grace of God. Nicholas' most holy uncle, the Archimandrite Nicholas, joined to him the priest Konon, the overseer for the construction of the Church of Holy Sion, and took him to the blessed and most holy Archbishop Nicholas, so that the latter would ordain him reader. When the most holy Archbishop saw the features of the child, which were full of grace, he recognized in spirit that the child was to become the "chosen vessel" of the Lord, and he took and blessed him and ordained him to the rank of the readers without receiving of him anything at all for the act of ordination.

6. Ἐρχομένου δὲ τοῦ παιδίου ἀπὸ τῆς Μυρέων μητροπόλεως, ἀπῆλθεν ἐν τῷ μαρτυρίῳ τοῦ ἁγίου Ἰωάννου πρὸς
τὸν αὐτοῦ θεῖον· καὶ προσκυνήσας αὐτὸν ἐπὶ τὴν γῆν, ηὐ-
λογήθη παρ' αὐτοῦ. καὶ δέδωκεν αὐτῷ βιβλίον ἔχον τὴν
5 θείαν λειτουργίαν καὶ τὰς λοιπὰς εὐχάς, τοῦ ἐκμανθάνειν
αὐτό. ὁ δὲ καὶ αὖθις βαλὼν μετάνοιαν ἠξίου εὔξασθαι
αὐτῷ· 'Ὅπως διὰ τῶν ἁγίων σου εὐχῶν,' φησίν, 'ἀξιώσῃ
κἀμὲ ὁ δεσπότης Χριστὸς τῆς αὐτοῦ βασιλείας.' ταῦτα
ἀκούσας παρὰ τοῦ παιδὸς ὁ ὅσιος αὐτοῦ θεῖος Νικόλαος,
10 σύνδακρυς γενόμενος, προσηύξατο πρὸς τὸν θεόν,
λέγων· 'Ὁ θεὸς ἡμῶν ὁ πιστὸς ἐν ἐπαγγελίαις καὶ ἀμε-
ταβλήτοις χαρίσμασιν καὶ ἀκατάληπτος φιλανθρωπίᾳ, ὁ
καλέσας τὸ πλάσμα σου κλήσει ἁγίᾳ καὶ συναγαγὼν τοὺς
δούλους σου εἰς τὴν ἀγγελικὴν ταύτην καὶ οὐράνιον ζωήν,
15 δὸς καὶ τούτῳ βίον εὐσχήμονα, πολιτείαν ἐνάρετον καὶ
ἀκατάγνωστον, καὶ πᾶσαν ἐργασίαν τῶν ἀρεσκόντων
σοι, ἵνα ἐν ἁγιασμῷ πολιτευσάμενος ἄξιος γένηται τῆς
λαμπρότητος τῶν ἁγίων καὶ τῆς βασιλείας τοῦ Χριστοῦ
σου.' καὶ ταῦτα αὐτοῦ εὐξαμένου τούτῳ, λέγει τῷ παιδίῳ·
20 'Τέκνον, σπούδασον τὸν ἀγῶνα τῆς ἐπαγγελίας καταλα-
βεῖν· ἐν σοὶ γὰρ ηὐδόκησεν ὁ θεὸς ἐν προσευχαῖς ἄρχειν
τοῦ ἐνδόξου οἴκου τῆς ἁγίας Σιών, καὶ διὰ σοῦ πολλοὶ
πιστεύσουσιν αὐτῷ.'

7. Ἰδὼν γὰρ ὁ ὁσιώτατος ἀρχιμανδρίτης Νικόλαος τὸ
ἔργον τοῦ ἐνδόξου οἴκου τῆς ἁγίας Σιὼν τέλειον ὑπάρχοντα διὰ τῆς τοῦ θεοῦ χάριτος καὶ τῆς τοῦ παιδὸς συν-
δρομῆς, ἐποίησεν αὐτὸν χειροτονηθῆναι πρεσβύτερον·
5 ἦν δὲ τότε ἐτῶν δεκαεννέα. καὶ μετὰ ταῦτα ἐγένετο τὰ
ἐγκαίνια τῆς ἁγίας Σιών. καὶ καταπιστευθεὶς παρὰ τοῦ

6. On his way back from the metropolis of Myra, the child came to the martyrium of St. John, to his uncle. And he bowed to the ground before him and was blessed by him. And the uncle gave him the book, which contained the Divine Liturgy and other prayers, for him to study. The youth bowed deeply again, and requested that his uncle pray on his behalf, "So that through your holy prayers," he said, "Christ the Lord may deem me, too, worthy of His Kingdom." When his holy uncle and spiritual father Nicholas heard this from the youth, he shed tears and prayed to God saying: "O our God, Thou Who art faithful in promises, steadfast in Thy gifts of grace and infinite in Thy love of man, Who hast summoned Thy handiwork through [Thy] summons, and hast gathered Thy servants for this angelic and heavenly life, give him the becoming life and virtuous and blameless ways, and may he be pleasing to Thee in all his works; so that, after a life of holiness, he may become worthy of the splendor of the saints and of the Kingdom of Thy Christ." Having thus prayed for him, he said to the child, "My child, strive to take up the struggle of the [monastic] profession, since it has pleased God that you should rule over the glorious shrine of Holy Sion in prayers; and through you many will come to believe in Him."

7. When the most holy Archimandrite Nicholas saw that the work on the glorious shrine of Holy Sion was completed by the grace of God and the assistance of the youth, he had him consecrated priest. The youth was then nineteen years old. Afterwards came the dedication of Holy

27

αὐτοῦ θείου τὸν ἔνδοξον οἶκον, καὶ μὴ ὄντων κληρικῶν,
ὁ φιλάνθρωπος θεός, ὁ ποιητὴς οὐρανοῦ καὶ γῆς, ἐδωρή-
10 σατο αὐτῷ τὴν πρὸς αὐτὸν ἀγωνίζεσθαι πίστιν· καὶ τὴν
ἐκ θεοῦ ἐλπίδα ἐσχηκώς, προσελάβετο αὐτῷ μαθητὰς
τοὺς αὐτοῦ ἀδελφούς, Ἀρτεμᾶν καὶ Ἑρμαῖον, πρὸς δια-
κονίαν καὶ τάξης [sic ms] ὑπηρεσίαν τῆς ἁγίας ἐκκλησίας
Σιών. κατέστησεν δὲ Ἀρτεμᾶν τὸν αὐτοῦ ἀδελφὸν
15 πρεσβύτερον καὶ δευτεράριον εἶναι, καὶ ἄρχειν τῆς ἁγίας
Σιών.

8. Μιᾷ οὖν τῶν ἡμερῶν ἔλαβεν αὐτὸν πόθος τοῦ κατελθεῖν εἰς τὴν ἁγίαν πόλιν καὶ προσκυνῆσαι τὸ τίμιον ξύλον
9Α   τοῦ τιμίου σταυροῦ καὶ πάντας τοὺς ἁγίους τόπους. καὶ
κατελθὼν ἐν Μύροις τῇ [τῆς ms] μητροπόλει, ἀπέρχεται
5 ἐν τῷ μαρτυρίῳ τοῦ ἁγίου καὶ ἐνδόξου Νικολάου. καὶ
θελήματι θεοῦ ἦν ναύκληρός τις ἀπὸ Ἀσκάλωνος, ὀνόματι Μηνᾶς. καὶ ἀκούσας τὰ περὶ τοῦ ὁσίου ἀνδρὸς Νικολάου, ἔρχεται εἰς ἀπάντησιν αὐτοῦ ἐν Μύροις, ἐν τῷ
μαρτυρίῳ τοῦ ἁγίου Νικολάου, καὶ λέγει αὐτῷ· ''Ἀκή-
10 κοα, ὅτι ἡ ὁσιότης ὑμῶν πλεῦσαι θέλει εἰς προσκύνησιν
τῆς ἁγίας πόλεως Ἰερουσαλὴμ καὶ τῆς τοῦ τιμίου σταυροῦ ἀπολαῦσαι δυνάμεως. καὶ εἰ κελεύει ἡ σὴ ἁγιωσύνη,
εἴσελθε ἐν τῷ πλοιαρίῳ μου καὶ εὐλόγησον ἡμᾶς.' λέγει
δὲ ὁ δοῦλος τοῦ θεοῦ Νικόλαος· Εἰ ποιεῖς τὴν φιλαν-
15 θρωπίαν τοῦ θεοῦ, ἀνέρχομαι μετὰ πάσης χαρᾶς.' καὶ
ηὔξατο λέγων· '«Ὁ θεὸς ὁ αἰώνιος, ὁ τῶν κρυπτῶν
γνώστης,» ὁ τὰ πάντα πρὶν γενέσεως ἐπιστάμενος, κύριε Ἰησοῦ Χριστέ, ἐπάκουσόν μου τοῦ ἁμαρτωλοῦ, καὶ
δὸς ἡμῖν ἐν τῷ ὀνόματί σου ἐπιτήδειον ἄνεμον, ἵνα περά-
20 σωμεν τὸ πέλαγος τῆς θαλάσσης καὶ δοξάσωμεν τὸ ὄνομά σου εἰς τοὺς αἰῶνας. ἀμήν.'

Sion and his uncle entrusted him with the glorious shrine. There being no clerics, God, Lover of mankind, Maker of heaven and earth, made him the gift of the faith to strive for Him; and having received hope from God, he joined to himself his brothers Artemas and Hermaios as disciples, for the ministry and carrying out of the rituals in the holy Church of Sion. He appointed his brother Artemas to be presbyter and *deuterarios* and to rule over Holy Sion.

8. One day he was seized by a desire to go down to the Holy City, to adore the venerable wood of the Holy Cross, and all the Holy Places. And going down to the metropolis of Myra, he went off to the martyrium of the glorious Saint Nicholas. And by the will of God, there was there a certain skipper from Askalon, by the name of Menas. And hearing reports about the holy man Nicholas, he came to meet him in Myra, in the martyrium of Saint Nicholas, and said to him; "I have heard that Your Holiness is about to sail on a pilgrimage to the Holy City of Jerusalem to reap benefit from the power of the Venerable Cross. And if it pleases Your Holiness, come aboard my little boat and bless us [by your presence]." The servant of God Nicholas said: "If you [thus] implement God's love towards men, I'll come aboard with great joy." And he prayed, saying: "'O eternal God, Who knowest the hidden things,' Who hast understood everything before creation, Lord Jesus Christ, hear me the sinner, and give us in Thy name a favorable wind, so that we may cross the open sea, and glorify Thy name forever. Amen."

9. Θελήματι δὲ θεοῦ κατήλθομεν ἐν τῷ λιμένι τῷ καλουμένῳ Ἀνδριάκῃ, καὶ εἰσελθόντες ἐν τῷ πλοίῳ τῇ τοῦ
θεοῦ χάριτι, ἀνέμου ἐπιτηδείου πνεύσαντος, διὰ πέντε
ἡμερῶν κατηντήσαμεν εἰς Ἀσκάλωνα. ἀνέβημεν οὖν εἰς
5 τὴν ἁγίαν πόλιν τοῦ Χριστοῦ, καὶ προσκυνήσαντες τὸν
10Α τίμιον σταυρὸν καὶ πάντας τοὺς ἁγίους τόπους, ἀπελθόντες ἕως τοῦ τιμίου Ἰορδάνου, καὶ τελειωσάντων
ἡμῶν τὴν εὐχὴν τῆς προσκυνήσεως τοῦ τιμίου σταυροῦ
καὶ τῆς Ἀναστάσεως τοῦ κυρίου ἡμῶν Ἰησοῦ Χριστοῦ,
10 θελήσει τοῦ θεοῦ καταπλεύσαντες, ἤλθαμεν ἐν τῇ Λυκίᾳ
ἐν τῇ Τραγλασσῶν κώμῃ.

10. Καὶ μετὰ ταῦτα ἦν ὁ μακάριος καὶ ὅσιος Νικόλαος
ἐν πολλῇ φροντίδι. ἔλεγεν δὲ πρὸς τοὺς αὐτοῦ ἀδελφοὺς
καὶ πρὸς πάντα τὸν λαόν· Οὗτός ἐστιν ὁ τόπος, ὅν μοι
ἔδειξεν ὁ θεὸς οἰκῆσαι καὶ κτίσαι. λοιπὸν ἀνδρίζεσθε
5 καὶ εὔχεσθε ὅπως ὁ κύριος ἀξίους ἡμᾶς ποιήσῃ δουλεῦ-
σαι τῇ αὐτοῦ εὐσπλαγχνίᾳ.' ἤρξατο δὲ οἰκοδομεῖν τὸν
ἔνδοξον οἶκον τοῦ εὐκτηρίου. οὕτως γὰρ ἠγάπησεν τὸν
τόπον ἐκεῖνον ὥσπερ τὸν παράδεισον τοῦ θεοῦ. ἐφάνη
γὰρ αὐτῷ ἄγγελος τοῦ κυρίου λέγων· Οὗτος ὁ τόπος
10 ἐστὶν ἀντίτυπος τῆς ἁγίας Σιὼν Ἰερουσαλήμ.'

11. Καὶ ἦν εὐχαριστῶν ὁ δοῦλος τοῦ θεοῦ Νικόλαος καθ'
ἑκάστην ἡμέραν, λέγων ἡμῖν ὅτι· Ἐπ' ἀληθείας οἶδα,
τέκνα μου, ὅτι οὗτος ὁ τόπος ἐστὶν ὁ τῆς καταπαύσεώς
μου. καὶ γὰρ ἐξ ἀρχῆς ἠγάπησα τὸν τόπον τοῦτον, ὅτι
5 πολλὰ σημεῖα ἐδείκνυεν ὁ θεὸς τοῖς δούλοις αὐτοῦ. τὸ
γὰρ φῶς τῆς ἁγίας Σιὼν προέλαμπεν ἐν τῷ τόπῳ ἐκείνῳ καὶ ἐν ἡμέρᾳ καὶ ἐν νυκτί. ἦν γάρ τις δοῦλος τοῦ θεοῦ,
ὀνόματι Σαββάτιος, ἐν τῷ Ἀκαλισσέῳ, καὶ τούτῳ πρώ-
10 τῳ ἐσήμανεν τὸ φῶς τοῦ τόπου τούτου. ἔλεγεν γὰρ πᾶσιν

9. By the will of God, we went down to the harbor called Andriake. We boarded the ship and there being a favorable wind by the grace of God, we got down to Askalon within five days. We then went up to the Holy City of Christ, and adored the Venerable Cross and all the Holy Places; we [even] went as far as the venerable Jordan. We fulfilled the vow of worshiping the Venerable Cross and the Church of the Resurrection of our Lord Jesus Christ, and by the will of God we sailed home, and came to Lycia to the village of Traglassos.

10. And after this, the blessed and holy Nicholas showed signs of great preoccupation. He said to his brethren and to all the people: "This is the place which God showed me to settle and build. So take courage, and pray that the Lord in His compassion shall make us worthy of serving Him." He began to build the glorious shrine. For he loved this spot as greatly as if it were God's paradise. For there had appeared to him an angel of the Lord, saying: "This spot is a counterpart of Holy Sion in Jerusalem."

11. And the servant of the Lord Nicholas gave thanks every day, saying to us: "I know in truth, my children, that this spot will be the place of my final rest. For even from the beginning, I loved this spot, since the Lord had been showing many signs to his servants. For the light of Holy Sion shone forth in that spot both by day and by night. For there had been a certain servant of God, Sabbatios by name, in the Akalissos [Monastery], and it was to him that

31

11Α ἀνθρώποις τὰ φαινόμενα αὐτῷ ἐν τῷ τόπῳ τούτῳ, πρὶν
ἢ γεννηθῆναί με Νικόλαον τὸν ἁμαρτωλόν. καὶ οὐδεὶς
ἐπίστευεν αὐτῷ· αὐτὸς δὲ ἔλεγεν αὐτοῖς ὅτι· «θεωρῶ
ὥσπερ λύχνον καιόμενον καὶ τὸ κτίσμα μονόλιθον, καὶ
15 ὅλον τὸ ὄρος λάμπον ἦν ὡς ὁ ἥλιος».'

12. Πολλὰ δὲ καὶ ἕτερα σημεῖα ἐθεώρουν οἱ δοῦλοι τοῦ
θεοῦ Σαββάτιος καὶ Νικόλαος ἐν ὁράματι, καὶ αὐτοπτικῶς ἐφαίνετο αὐτοῖς ἡ ἁγία Σιών. χρόνου δὲ παρελθόν-
τος ἐκοιμήθη ὁ προλεχθεὶς ὁσιώτατος Σαββάτιος. ὁ δὲ
5 δευτεράριος αὐτοῦ καὶ δοῦλος τοῦ θεοῦ Νικόλαος ηὔχε-
το καθ᾽ ἑκάστην ἡμέραν κυρίῳ τῷ θεῷ, ὅπως ὁ κύριος
Ἰησοῦς Χριστὸς φανερώσῃ τὸ σημεῖον τὸ ὀφθὲν τῷ ὁσίῳ
Σαββατίῳ. εἶχεν γὰρ τὴν πύρωσιν τοῦ ἁγίου πνεύματος,
εὐχόμενός τε καὶ παρακαλῶν τὸν θεόν, ὅπως φανερωθῇ
10 τὸ ποθούμενον αὐτῷ, τὰ περὶ τῆς ἁγίας καὶ ἐνδόξου
Σιών.

13. Καὶ ἐξαπέστειλεν κύριος ὁ θεὸς Μιχαὴλ τὸν ἀρχάγγελον τῆς διαθήκης, αὐτοπτικῶς λέγοντα τῷ δούλῳ τοῦ
θεοῦ Νικολάῳ· ῾Θέλεις θεωρῆσαι τερπνὸν τὸν οἶκον τῆς
ἁγίας Σιών;' καὶ λέγει αὐτῷ· ῾Ναί, κύριε.' λέγει αὐτῷ ὁ
5 τοῦ θεοῦ ἀρχιστράτηγος· ῾Δεῦρο, ἀκολούθει μοι, καὶ
ὄψει τὸν οἶκον τοῦ θεοῦ κτισμένον.' ῾Καὶ ἤγαγέν με εἰς
12Α τὸ ὄρος τοῦτο, καὶ λέγει μοι· «Βλέψον εἰς τὸ ὄρος.» καὶ
ἀναβλέψας εἶδον τὸν οἶκον τοῦ θεοῦ κτισμένον ἐν πάσῃ
εὐπρεπείᾳ, καὶ φῶς μέγα ἔλαμψεν ἐν τῷ ὄρει τούτῳ. καὶ
10 λέγει μοι ὁ ἄγγελος ὁ ὁδηγῶν με· «῎Εστιν παιδίον ὧδε,
ὀνόματι Νικόλαος, υἱὸς Ἐπιφανίου, μητρὸς δὲ Νόννας,
ὃς ἔχει οἰκῆσαι ἐν τῷ τόπῳ τούτῳ καὶ δοξάσαι τὸν πατέ-
ρα ἡμῶν τὸν ἐν τοῖς οὐρανοῖς. ἐκ κοιλίας γὰρ μητρός
ἐστιν ἐκλελεγμένος παρὰ τῷ θεῷ.» καὶ ἀφανὴς ἐγένετο

the light of this place was first manifested. For he told to all men what was appearing to him in this place, before I, Nicholas the sinner, was ever born. And no one believed him. He said to them: 'I see, as it were, a burning light, and a structure made all of stone and the whole mountain shining like the sun.'"

12. Many other signs as well did the servants of God Sabbatios and Nicholas [the Elder] witness in visions, and Holy Sion appeared to them before their very eyes. After some time, the aforementioned most holy Sabbatios passed away. His *deuterarios*, the servant of God Nicholas, prayed each day to the Lord God, that the Lord Jesus Christ would reveal the sign which had been seen by holy Sabbatios. For having the flame of the Holy Spirit in him, he prayed and besought God, that the object of his desire should be revealed to him, namely, the things concerning the holy and glorious Sion.

13. And the Lord God dispatched Michael, the archangel of the Covenant, who appeared face to face to the servant of God Nicholas [the Elder] and said: "Do you wish to set eyes upon the delightful shrine of Holy Sion?" And he said to him: "Yea, Lord." The leader of the Lord's hosts said to him; "Here, follow me, and you will see the shrine of God built." "And he led me to this mountain, and said to me: 'Look at the mountain.' And looking up, I saw the shrine of God built in all seemliness, and a great light shone on this mountain. And the angel who was guiding me said: 'There is a child here, by the name of Nicholas, son of Epiphanios, his mother being Nonna, who will dwell in this place, and glorify our Father which is in Heaven. For

15 ὁ ἄγγελος ἀπ᾽ ἐμοῦ.᾽ ταῦτα ἔλεγεν ὁ δοῦλος τοῦ θεοῦ
Νικόλαος, ὁ ἀρχιμανδρίτης τῆς μονῆς τοῦ ἁγίου Ἰωάννου ἐν τῷ Ἀκαλισσέῳ, προφητεύων τὰ περὶ τοῦ ὁσίου
παιδίου. καὶ ἐγένετο ἡ κατάπαυσις αὐτοῦ ἐν τῷ Ἀκαλισσέῳ, ἔνδον τοῦ ἁγίου Ἰωάννου.

14. Αὐξηθέντος δὲ τοῦ ὁσίου παιδίου καὶ καταπιστευθέν-
τος ἀπὸ τοῦ ἁγίου πνεύματος τὸν ἔνδοξον οἶκον τῆς
ἁγίας Σιών, ἔλαβεν τὴν τοῦ ἁγίου πνεύματος παρρησίαν,
καὶ πολλὰ σημεῖα καὶ ἰάσεις παρέσχεν τοῖς πιστεύουσιν
5 δι᾽ αὐτοῦ τῇ ἁγίᾳ Σιών.

15. Μιᾷ δὲ τῶν ἡμερῶν ἦλθόν τινες προσπίπτοντες τῷ
ὁσίῳ Νικολάῳ ἀπὸ τῆς Πλακωμιτῶν κώμης λέγοντες·
ʽΔοῦλε τοῦ θεοῦ, ἔστιν ἐν τῷ ἡμετέρῳ κτήματι ξύλον
ἱερόν, ἐφ᾽ ᾧ ἐνοικεῖ πνεῦμα εἰδώλου ἀκαθάρτου, καὶ
5 ἀφανίζει τοὺς ἀνθρώπους καὶ τὸν ἀγρόν· †κάταστρον†
13A γάρ ἐστιν καὶ τῇ χώρᾳ, καὶ οὐ δυνάμεθα καλῶς διαπρά-
ξασθαι ἐξ αὐτοῦ. παρακληθεῖσα οὖν ἡ ὑμῶν ὁσιότης ἀξιώσῃ παραγενέσθαι σὺν ἡμῖν καὶ ἐκκόψαι αὐτό, ὅπως
ὁ φιλάνθρωπος θεὸς διὰ τῶν εὐχῶν σου ἀποδιώξῃ τὸ
10 ἀκάθαρτον πνεῦμα τὸ ἐνοικοῦν ἐν αὐτῷ τῷ ξύλῳ, καὶ
εἰρήνευσαντες ἄνεσιν λάβῃ ὁ ἀγρὸς σὺν τῇ χώρᾳ᾽.

16. Παρακληθεὶς δὲ ὁ δοῦλος τοῦ θεοῦ Νικόλαος πλεῖ-
στα παρὰ τῶν οἰκούντων τὴν Πλακωμιτῶν κώμην,
προσευξάμενος ἐπέστη τῷ τόπῳ, οὗ ἦν τὸ ξύλον ἑστῶτα.
ἰδὼν δὲ ὁ ὅσιος Νικόλαος τὸ ξύλον λέγει· ʽΤοῦτό ἐστιν
5 τὸ ἱερὸν ξύλον;᾽ ἀποκριθέντες δὲ οἱ ἄνδρες τοῦ προλε-
χθέντος ἀγροῦ λέγουσιν αὐτῷ· ʽΝαί, κύριε.᾽ καὶ λέγει
ὁ δοῦλος τοῦ θεοῦ Νικόλαος· ʽΤί ἐστιν ἡ κοπὰς ἡ οὖσα

from his mother's womb was he chosen by God.' And the angel vanished from my sight.'' So spoke the servant of God, Nicholas, the archimandrite of the Monastery of Saint John in Akalissos, prophesying about the holy child. And he was laid to rest in Akalissos, within the [Monastery] of Saint John.

14. The holy child grew up, and was entrusted by the Holy Spirit with the glorious shrine of Holy Sion; he received boldness from the Holy Spirit, and produced many [miraculous] signs and cures for those who believed through him in Holy Sion.

15. One day there came men from the village of Plakoma, who fell down before holy Nicholas and said: ''O servant of God, on our land there is a sacred tree in which dwells the spirit of an unclean idol, that destroys both men and fields. It is also . . . .to the district and we are unable to go unhindered about our business [?] on account of it. May Your Holiness yield to our entreaties and deign to come with us and fell it, so that God, Lover of mankind, may through your prayers drive out the unclean spirit dwelling in that tree, and the fields and the district may be at peace and find respite.''

16. Being so strongly urged by the inhabitants of the village of Plakoma, Nicholas, the servant of God, offered prayers, and came to the spot where the tree stood. Seeing the tree, holy Nicholas said: ''Is this the sacred tree?'' In response, the men of the aforementioned fields said to him: ''Yes, Lord.'' And Nicholas the servant of God said: ''What are those gashes

ἐν τῷ ξύλῳ;᾽ λέγουσιν αὐτῷ ὅτι· 'Τίς τῶν ἀρχαίων ἦλθεν
κόψαι τὸ ξύλον μετὰ δύο ἀξινῶν καὶ ἑνὸς πέλυκος. καὶ
10 ὡς ἤρξατο κόπτειν αὐτό, τὸ ἀκάθαρτον πνεῦμα ἐξήρπα-
σεν τὰ ξίφη καὶ ἐψόφισεν τὸν ἄνθρωπον, ὡς καὶ τὴν
ταφὴν αὐτοῦ εὑρεθῆναι πρὸς τὴν ῥίζαν τοῦ δένδρου.᾽
προσευξάμενος δὲ ὁ δοῦλος τοῦ θεοῦ Νικόλαος, παρε-
στώτων πλῆθος ἀνδρῶν τε καὶ γυναικῶν καὶ παιδίων
15 ὡσεὶ τριακοσίων ἐπὶ τὸ θεωρῆσαι τὴν τοῦ θεοῦ δημιουρ-
γίαν—οὐ γὰρ ἐπείθοντο πάντες, ὅτι τοιοῦτον ξύλον ἱερὸν
ὑπάρχοντα μέλλει κόπτεσθαι—, τότε ὁ δοῦλος τοῦ θεοῦ
Νικόλαος, κλίνας τὰ γόνατα, προσηύξατο ἐπὶ ὥρας δύο.
καὶ ἀναστὰς ἐπέτρεψεν τοῖς συμπαρεστῶσιν ἀνδράσι
14Α20 λέγων· ''Εν τῷ ὀνόματι τοῦ κυρίου ἡμῶν Ἰησοῦ Χριστοῦ
καὶ τῆς ἁγίας Σιών, δεῦτε, ἐπιχειρήσατε κόπτειν αὐτό.᾽

17. Τρόμος δὲ ἔλαβεν πάντας τοὺς παρεστῶτας τῷ ὁσίῳ
Νικολάῳ, ὡς μηδὲ θεωρεῖν τολμῆσαι τὸ ξύλον. τότε ἔφη
ὁ δοῦλος τοῦ θεοῦ Νικόλαος· 'Δότε μοι τὸ ξίφος, κἀγὼ
ἐν τῷ ὀνόματι τοῦ κυρίου μου κόπτω αὐτό.᾽ λαβόμενος
5 δὲ τὸ ξίφος ὁ δοῦλος τοῦ θεοῦ Νικόλαος καὶ σφραγίσας,
ἔδωκεν τῷ ἱερῷ ξύλῳ πληγὰς ἑπτά. ἰδόντα δὲ τὸ ἀκάθαρτον πνεῦμα, ὅτι τὴν τοῦ θεοῦ ἐξουσίαν ἔχει ὁ δοῦλος
τοῦ θεοῦ Νικόλαος, πληγέντος τοῦ ξύλου ὑπὸ τῶν ὁσίων
αὐτοῦ χειρῶν, ἀνέκραγεν τὸ ἀκάθαρτον πνεῦμα λέ-
10 γοντα· 'Οὐαί μοι, ὅτι τὴν τοσαύτην αὔξησιν τῆς κατοι-
κίας μου ἐθέμην ἐν τῷ ξύλῳ τούτῳ τῆς κυπαρίσσου, μη-
δέποτε ὑπό τινος νικηθείς· καὶ νῦν ὁ δοῦλος τοῦ θεοῦ
Νικόλαος φυγαδεύει με, ὡς μηκέτι ὀφθῆναί με ἐν τῷ
τόπῳ τούτῳ. οὐ μόνον γὰρ ὅτι ἐκ τῆς παροικίας τοῦ ἐμοῦ
15 δένδρου ἐξήγαγέν με, ἀλλὰ καὶ ἐκ τῶν μεθορίων τῆς
Λυκίας σὺν τῇ ἁγίᾳ Σιὼν διώκει με.᾽

in the tree?'' They said to him: "Some man of old came to fell the tree with two hatchets, and an axe. And as he began to fell it, the unclean spirit snatched away the blades, and slaughtered the man, so that his grave was found at the roots of the tree.'' Offering prayers, the servant of God Nicholas—there being a crowd of nearly three hundred men, women and children to watch the workings of God, for none believed that such a tree, being sacred, was about to be felled—then the servant of God Nicholas knelt and prayed for two hours. And rising, he enjoined the men around saying: "In the name of our Lord Jesus Christ and of Holy Sion, come here, try and cut it down.''

17. A shiver ran through all those who were standing around holy Nicholas, and no one dared so much as to look at the tree. Then the servant of God Nicholas said: "Give me the blade and I will cut it down myself in the name of my Lord." Taking the blade, the servant of God Nicholas made the sign of the cross over it and struck the sacred tree seven times. The unclean spirit saw that the servant of God Nicholas had power from God, and when the tree was struck by Nicholas' holy hands, the unclean spirit cried out, saying: "Woe be unto me: I made for myself an ever-expanding dwelling in this cypress tree and have never been overcome by anyone; and now the servant of God Nicholas is putting me to flight, and no longer will I be seen in this place. For not only has he expelled me from my dwelling in the tree, but he is driving me from the confines of Lycia, with the help of Holy Sion.''

18. Τελειουμένης δὲ τῆς ἐκκόψεως τοῦ τοιούτου ἱεροῦ
ξύλου, λέγει ὁ δοῦλος τοῦ θεοῦ Νικόλαος· 'Συνάχθητε
πάντες ὁμοθυμαδὸν κατὰ τοῦ ἀνάβου ἐπὶ ἄρκτον.' συνο-
ρᾶτο γὰρ ἡ πτῶσις τοῦ ἱεροῦ ξύλου ἐπὶ δυσμάς. τὸ δὲ
5 ἀκάθαρτον πνεῦμα ἐνόμιζεν ἐν τῇ ὥρᾳ ἐκείνῃ ἐκφοβεῖν
τὸν ὄχλον. καὶ ἔνευσεν τὸ ξύλον κατὰ ἄρκτον ἐπὶ τοῦ
ἀνάβου, ὅπου ἵστατο ὁ ὄχλος θεωρῶν, ὡς πάντας φοβη-
θέντας κράζειν μιᾷ τῇ φωνῇ, λέγοντας· 'Δοῦλε τοῦ θεοῦ,
τὸ ξύλον ἐπάνωθεν ἡμῶν ὥρμησεν, καὶ ἀπολλύμεθα.' ὁ
10 δὲ δοῦλος τοῦ θεοῦ Νικόλαος, σφραγίσας τὸ ξύλον καὶ
15A ἀντιβὰς ταῖς δύο χερσίν, λέγει τῷ ἱερῷ ξύλῳ· ''Εν τῷ
ὀνόματι τοῦ κυρίου μου Ἰησοῦ Χριστοῦ κελεύω σοι· ὑπό-
στρεψον εἰς τὰ ὀπίσω, καὶ ὕπαγε, ὅπου ὥρισέν σοι ὁ
θεός.' θελήματι δὲ τοῦ θεοῦ εὐθέως ἀνέκαμψεν τὸ ξύλον
15 καὶ ὥρμησεν ἐπὶ δυσμάς, ὅπου ἡ πτῶσις αὐτοῦ ἐγένετο.
ἀπὸ δὲ τῆς ὥρας ἐκείνης οὐκέτι ὤφθη τὸ ἀκάθαρτον
πνεῦμα ἐν τοῖς ὁρίοις ἐκείνοις. καὶ ἐδόξασαν τὸν θεὸν
πάντες λέγοντες· 'Εἷς θεός, ὁ δώσας ἐξουσίαν τῷ δούλῳ
αὐτοῦ κατὰ τῶν ἀκαθάρτων πνευμάτων.'

19. Κοπέντος δὲ τοῦ ἱεροῦ ξύλου, ὁ δοῦλος τοῦ θεοῦ ἐδήλωσεν ἐν τῇ Μυρέων μητροπόλει ἐπὶ τῷ εὑρεῖν τεχνίτας
καὶ πρισθῆναι τὸ ξύλον. ἀκούσαντες δὲ οἱ τεχνῖται τὸ
μέγεθος τοῦ ξύλου, ὅτι οὐ μόνον τὸ πάχος ἔσχεν ἡ τομὴ
5 αὐτοῦ πηχῶν τριῶν ἡμίσεως, ἀλλὰ καὶ τὸ ὕψος πηχῶν
τεσσαράκοντα, ἐδειλίασαν *οἱ τεχνῖται* ὅτι· 'Οὐκ ἂν πε-
ριγίνεσθαι < ἰσχ >ύωμεν τοῦ τοιούτου ξύλου.' ἐδήλωσεν
δὲ ὁ δοῦλος τοῦ θεοῦ Νικόλαος εὑρίσκεσθαι κατὰ πᾶσαν
πόλιν τεχνίτας. καὶ μὴ εὑρηκώς, ἠναγκάσθη δηλῶσαι ἐν
10 τῇ Καρκαβιωτῶν κώμῃ. καὶ εὑρέθησαν τεχνῖται ὀνόματα
πέντε, καὶ τῇ τοῦ θεοῦ δυνάμει καὶ ταῖς εὐχαῖς τοῦ ὁσίου

18. When he was about to fell this sacred tree, the servant of God said: "Assemble with one accord up the slope on the North side." For it was expected that the tree would fall to the West. The unclean spirit thought at that moment to frighten the crowd. And he made the tree lean toward the North, up the slope where the crowd stood watching, so that they all screamed with fear in one voice, saying: "Servant of God, the tree is coming down on top of us, and we will perish." The servant of God Nicholas made the sign of the cross over the tree, pushed it back with his two hands, and said to the sacred tree: "In the name of my Lord Jesus Christ I command you: turn back [in the other direction] and go down where God has ordained you." Forthwith, the tree swayed back by the will of God and moved toward the West, where it crashed. From that time on, the unclean spirit was no longer seen within those parts. And they all glorified God, saying: "One is God, who gave power to his servant against the unclean spirits."

19. The sacred tree having been felled, the servant of God gave instructions in the metropolis of Myra that workmen be found to saw up the tree. When the workmen heard of the size of the tree, that not only was its stump the thickness of three and a half cubits but that its height was forty cubits, they were afraid, saying: "We will not be able to cope with such a tree." So the servant of God Nicholas made it known that he was seeking workmen from any city. And finding none, he was forced to make his announcement in the village of Karkabo. And workmen were found, five in number, and by the power of God and the prayers of holy Nicholas, they sawed up the tree. When the whole

Νικολάου τὴν πρισμὴν τοῦ ξύλου ἐποιήσαντο. ἰδοῦσα
δὲ πᾶσα ἡ περίχωρος τῆς Ἀρνεατῶν καὶ Μυρέων ἐνορίας, ὅτι διὰ τῶν εὐχῶν τοῦ ὁσίου Νικολάου ἐπρίσθη
15 τὸ ξύλον, ἤρχοντο ἐξ εὐχῆς σύρειν αὐτό. συρθὲν δὲ ἦλθεν
16Α ἐν τῷ ἁγίῳ καὶ ἐνδόξῳ οἴκῳ τῆς ἁγίας Σιών. καὶ πάντες
ἐδόξαζον τὸν θεόν, τὸν δώσαντα τοιαύτην ἐξουσίαν τῷ
δούλῳ αὐτοῦ Νικολάῳ.

20. Ἀκούσαντες δὲ οἱ ἐκ τῆς Ἀρναβανδέων κώμης τὴν
πίστιν τοῦ ἀββᾶ Νικολάου, εἶπον ἐν αὐτοῖς· ʽΔεῦτε,
πάντες ἀπελθόντες προσκυνήσωμεν αὐτῷ καὶ ἀπαγγεί-
λωμεν αὐτῷ πάντα, ὅσα συνέβη ἐπὶ ταῖς πηγαῖς τῶν ὑδά-
5 των ἡμῶν.ʼ ἐλθόντων δὲ τῶν κληρικῶν τῆς Ἀρναβανδέων κώμης ἐν τῷ ἁγίῳ μοναστηρίῳ τῆς ἁγίας Σιών,
προσέπεσαν τῷ δούλῳ τοῦ θεοῦ Νικολάῳ, λέγοντες·
ʽΔεόμεθά σου, κελεύσῃ ἡ σὴ ἁγιωσύνη ἐλθεῖν ἐν τῇ κώμῃ ἡμῶν καὶ προσεύξασθαι περὶ ἡμῶν, ὅτι πάνυ ὁ διά-
10 βολος πειράζει ἡμᾶς. εἴχομεν γὰρ ἀρχαίαν πηγήν, καὶ
ἐξῆλθεν γυνὴ τοῦ ὑδρεύσασθαι, καὶ τὸ ἀκάθαρτον πνεῦμα ἔρριψεν αὐτὴν εἰς τὴν πηγήν, καὶ ἀπέθανεν. καὶ κινδυνεύομεν ἡμεῖς πάντες σὺν τοῖς τετραπόδοις ἡμῶν· ἐτα-
ράχθη γὰρ ἀπὸ τῆς ὥρας ἐκείνης τὸ ὕδωρ καὶ ἐγένετο
15 βεβορβορωμένον. καὶ δειλία ἡμᾶς κατέσχεν, καὶ οὐδεὶς
ἐγγίζει ἔτι τῇ πηγῇ ἐκείνῃ, καὶ ἀποθνήσκομεν σὺν τοῖς
τετραπόδοις ἡμῶν. λέγει ὁ δοῦλος τοῦ θεοῦ Νικόλαος·
ʽʽἘὰν πιστεύητε εἰς τὸν κύριόν μου Ἰησοῦν Χριστόν,
ἀνέρχομαι πρὸς ὑμᾶς, καὶ ἀπερχόμεθα πρὸς τὴν πηγήν,
20 καὶ ἔχει ὁ κύριός μου Ἰησοῦς Χριστὸς διὰ τῶν πρε-
σβειῶν τῶν ἁγίων εὐλογῆσαι τὸ ὕδωρ.ʼ λέγουσιν δὲ οἱ
ἄνδρες τῆς χώρας ἐκείνης· ʽʽἩμεῖς πιστεύομεν εἰς τὸν
θεὸν καὶ εἰς τὴν σὴν ἁγιωσύνην, ὅτι, ἐὰν θέλῃς παρακαλέσαι κύριον τὸν θεόν, πάντα ὅσα ἐὰν αἰτήσῃς τὸν θεόν,
25 ἐπακούει σου ὁ θεός· μεγάλην γὰρ πίστιν καὶ χάριν

surrounding district of Arneai and Myra saw that the tree had been sawed up by the prayers of holy Nicholas, they obtained his permission [?] and came to drag it away. It was dragged to the holy and glorious shrine of Holy Sion, and all glorified God, who had given such power unto His servant Nicholas.

20. And when the villagers of Arnabanda heard of the faith of Father Nicholas, they said to each other: "Look here, let us all go down and worship him and recount to him everything that has happened to our spring of water." So the clerics of the village of Arnabanda came to the holy Monastery of Holy Sion, fell down before Nicholas, the servant of God, and said: "We beg you, would it please Your Holiness, come to our village and pray for us, since the Devil has tried us sorely. For we had an old spring, and a woman went there to draw water, and the unclean spirit threw her into the spring and she died. And we are all in danger, along with our animals. For from that very hour the water was troubled and turned muddy. And we were overcome with fear, and no one still has gone near that spring, and we and our animals are dying." The servant of God Nicholas said: "if you believe in my Lord Jesus Christ, I will go up with you, and we will go out to the spring, and my Lord Jesus Christ, through the intercession of the saints, will bless the water." The men of that district said: "We believe in God and in Your Holiness that, whenever you will call upon the Lord God, whatever you may ask from God, God will listen to you. For God has

17A ἐδωρήσατό σοι ὁ θεός. καὶ ὡς ἔδειξας ἐπὶ τὸ ἱερὸν ξύλον
καὶ ἐφυγάδευσας τὸ ἀκάθαρτον πνεῦμα καὶ τὸ ἱερὸν εἰς
ἁγιασμὸν ἠλευθέρωσας καὶ εἰς φυλακτήριον τοῖς ἀνθρώποις, οὕτως καὶ ἐφ' ἡμᾶς τοὺς ἁμαρτωλοὺς ποίησον, ὅτι
30 πάνυ ἡμᾶς πειράζει ὁ μισόκαλος καὶ φθονερὸς διάβολος.'

21. Ἐξέρχεται οὖν ὁ δοῦλος τοῦ θεοῦ Νικόλαος τῇ τοῦ
θεοῦ δυνάμει, καὶ ἀπέρχεται ἐν Ἀρναβάνδοις τῇ κώμῃ.
συνήχθησαν δὲ οἱ ἄνδρες τῆς κώμης ἐκείνης ἀπὸ μικροῦ
ἕως μεγάλου, καὶ ἦραντο ⟨ τὸ ⟩ μεγαλεῖον καὶ τοὺς
5 τιμίους σταυρούς, καὶ ἦλθον εἰς ἀπάντησιν τοῦ δούλου
τοῦ θεοῦ Νικολάου, λέγοντες αὐτῷ· 'Καλῶς ἐλήλυθας,
δοῦλε τοῦ θεοῦ, ἐλέησον ἡμᾶς.' καὶ λέγει ὁ τοῦ θεοῦ
δοῦλος· 'Πιστεύετε, ὅτι δύναμαι ὑμᾶς σῶσαι ἢ ὠφελῆσαί
τι;' λέγουσιν αὐτῷ· 'Ναί, κύριε.' λέγει δὲ πρὸς αὐτοὺς
10 ὁ δοῦλος τοῦ θεοῦ· ''Απέλθωμεν πρῶτον ἐν τῇ ἁγίᾳ ἐκκλησίᾳ, καὶ γενέσθω σύναξις, καὶ ἔχει ὁ κύριος φανερῶσαί μοι τὰ περὶ ὑμῶν.' ἀπελθόντων δὲ αὐτῶν ἐν τῇ ἁγίᾳ
ἐκκλησίᾳ συνῆλθον πάντες ὁμοθυμαδόν. μετὰ δὲ τὴν
ἁγίαν σύναξιν ἐξέρχεται ὁ τοῦ θεοῦ δοῦλος Νικόλαος
15 καὶ καθέζεται πρὸς τὴν πύλην τῆς ἁγίας ἐκκλησίας. καὶ
λέγει παντὶ τῷ λαῷ· 'Ἐγώ, ἀδελφοί, ἄνθρωπός εἰμι ταπεινὸς καὶ ἁμαρτωλός· ὁ δὲ κύριός μου Ἰησοῦς Χρι-
στός, φιλάνθρωπος ὤν, ὅπως φανερώσῃ ἡμῖν τὴν δύναμιν αὐτοῦ.'

18A **22.** Τότε προσέπεσεν αὐτῷ ἄνθρωπος καὶ λέγει τῷ δούλῳ
τοῦ θεοῦ· ''Ελέησόν με, ἅγιε τοῦ θεοῦ, καὶ μὴ ποιήσῃς
μοι κατὰ τὴν ἀπιστίαν μου, ἀπολέσθαι με. ἐγὼ γάρ εἰμι
ἐν τῇ Καβαλείᾳ ἐν Ἀκαρασσῷ, καὶ ἔρχεταί τις τῆς γειτο-
5 νίας μου καὶ λέγει μοι ὅτι· «Κληρικοί τινες τῆς κώμης
ἡμῶν ἀπέρχονται πρὸς τὸν δίκαιον καὶ δοῦλον τοῦ θεοῦ

granted you great faith and grace. And as you did with respect to the sacred tree, when you put to flight the unclean spirit, and set the sacred [tree] free for sanctification, and for a protection for men, so also do unto us sinners, too, since the envious Devil, the hater of good, is trying us sorely.''

21. And so Nicholas, the servant of God, went out by the power of God and set out for the village of Arnabanda. The men of that village gathered together, young and old, and they took up the Gospel Book and the venerable crosses, and came to meet Nicholas, the servant of God, saying to him: "Welcome, servant of God, have mercy upon us." And the servant of God said: "Do you have faith that I am able to save you or help in some way?" They said to him: "Yea, Lord." The servant of God said to them: "Let us go first to the holy church, and let there be a service, and the Lord will reveal to me things concerning you." They went to the holy church, and all of them gathered of one accord. After the holy service, the servant of God Nicholas came outside and sat down by the door of the holy church. And he said to all the people: "I, brothers, am a lowly and sinful man. But my Lord Jesus Christ, who loves mankind, may He reveal His power to you."

22. Then a man fell down before him and said to the servant of God: "Have mercy on me, O holy man of God, and do not bring about my undoing according to my lack of faith. For I was in Kabaleia, in Akarassos, and there came a certain man from my neighborhood, who said to me: 'Some clerics from our village are going down to the

Νικόλαον ἐν τῇ ἁγίᾳ Σιών, ἵνα παρακαλέσωσιν αὐτόν,
ὅπως ἔλθῃ καὶ ἐλεήσῃ ἡμᾶς.» καὶ ἀπιστήσας ἐγὼ εἶπον
αὐτῷ· «Τίς ἐστιν δοῦλος τοῦ θεοῦ; ζῇ κύριος ὁ θεός, οὐκ
10 ἂν πιστεύσω ἀνθρώπῳ ἐπὶ τῆς γῆς.» ἰδὼν δὲ ὁ θεὸς τὴν
ἀπιστίαν μου, τῇ νυκτὶ ἐκείνῃ φαίνεταί μοι ποταμὸς πε-
πληρωμένος βορβόρου, πνίγων με διὰ τὴν ἀπιστίαν μου.
ἔκραξα δὲ φωνῇ μεγάλῃ καὶ εἶπον· «Ἐλέησόν με, κύριε,
καὶ ἐξάρπασόν με ἀπὸ τοῦ βορβόρου τούτου.» φωνὴ δὲ
19A15 ἐπέστη μοι ἐκ τῶν ὑψίστων λέγουσα· «Ἔρχεται πρὸς
σὲ ὁ δοῦλος τοῦ θεοῦ Νικόλαος, ὃς ἀναγάγῃ σε ἐκ τοῦ
βορβόρου τούτου.» καὶ εὐθέως ἐφάνης μοι, ἅγιε τοῦ θεοῦ,
τῇ αὐτῇ ὥρᾳ, καὶ ἐκτείνας τὴν χεῖρα κρατήσας ἀνήγα-
γές με ἐκ τοῦ βορβόρου λέγων· «Τέκνον, γίνου πιστὸς
20 καὶ μὴ ἄπιστος· τῶν γὰρ ἀπίστων ἀνθρώπων ἡ κρίσις
τοιαύτη ἐστίν.»' ταῦτα εἶπεν ὁ ἄνθρωπος ὁ τῇ ἀπιστίᾳ
κρατηθείς.

23. Ἔπειτα λέγουσιν τῷ δούλῳ τοῦ θεοῦ Νικολάῳ οἱ
κληρικοὶ τῆς κώμης Ἀρναβανδῶν· 'Κύριε, ἔστιν παρ'
ἡμῖν, ἐν τῷ ὄρει Καίσαρι, ὕδωρ κεκρυμμένον.' καὶ λέγει ὁ δοῦλος τοῦ θεοῦ· 'Μέμνησθέ ποτε ἀπὸ τῶν πατέρων
5 ὑμῶν, ὅτι ὡράθη ἐν τῷ ὄρει ἐκείνῳ τὸ ὕδωρ;' λέγουσιν
αὐτῷ ὅτι μέν· ''Ακοὴν ἠκούσαμεν, καὶ κατέχομεν τὴν
20A ὀνομασίαν, ὅτι ἔστιν ἐν τῷ ὄρει τούτῳ ὕδωρ, ἐπεὶ οὐδεὶς
ἐκ τῆς συγγενείας ἡμῶν οἶδεν ἢ ἐπίσταται.' καὶ λέγει ὁ
δοῦλος τοῦ θεοῦ· 'Ἐν τῷ ὀνόματι τοῦ κυρίου μου
10 Ἰησοῦ Χριστοῦ συναχθέντες πάντες ἀπὸ μικροῦ ἕως μεγάλου, καὶ ἄρωμεν εἰς τὰς χεῖρας ἡμῶν τὸ μεγαλεῖον
τοῦ θεοῦ μετὰ τῶν τιμίων σταυρῶν, καὶ προθύμως ἀπέλθωμεν ἐπὶ τὸν τόπον καὶ τὸν προκείμενον ἡμῖν ἀγῶνα
ποιήσωμεν, καὶ κύριος ὁ θεὸς φανερώσει τὸ αἴτημα
15 ὑμῶν.'

just Nicholas, the servant of God, to Holy Sion, in order to beseech him to come and have mercy on us.' And I lacked faith, and said to him: 'Who is the servant of God? God the Lord lives, and I would not believe in any man on earth.' God saw my lack of faith, and that night there appeared to me a river filled with mire, drowning me for my lack of faith. I cried with a loud voice and said: 'Have mercy on me, Lord, and extract me from this mire.' A voice came to me from on high, saying: 'The servant of God Nicholas will come to you, and he will lead you out of this mire.' And straightway you appeared to me, O holy man of God, that very moment, and extended your hand and took hold of me, and led me out of the mire, saying: 'My child, be believing, not faithless. For such is the sentence for faithless men.'" So spoke the man who had been overcome by lack of faith.

23. Then the clerics of the village of Arnabanda said to the servant of God Nicholas: "O Lord, there is in our vicinity, on Mount Kaisar, a hidden source of water." And the servant of God said: "Do you remember at all [hearing] from your fathers that water had been seen on that mountain?" They said to him: "We [only] heard reports, and it has been mentioned that there is water in that mountain, for no one of our kindred knows or has found out." And the servant of God said: "In the name of our Lord Jesus Christ, gather all of you, young and old, and let us take in our hands God's Gospel, with the venerable crosses, and let us go eagerly to the spot and perform the feat which lies before us, and Lord God will reveal what you have requested."

45

24. Ἐξελθόντες οὖν πάντες μετὰ τοῦ δούλου τοῦ θεοῦ
Νικολάου ἐπέστησαν ἐν τῷ τόπῳ τῷ καλουμένῳ Καίσαρι. ἰδὼν δὲ ὁ δοῦλος τοῦ θεοῦ τὸν τόπον λέγει αὐτοῖς·
'Πιστεύσατε εἰς τὸν θεόν, καὶ κάμωμεν ὀλίγον, καὶ κύ-
5 ριος ὁ θεὸς πληρώσει τὸ αἴτημα ὑμῶν.' καὶ ἔστη ἐν τῷ
τόπῳ ὁ ἅγιος, καὶ κλίνας τὰ γόνατα προσηύξατο πρὸς
τὸν θεὸν λέγων· 'Δέσποτά μου, κύριε Ἰησοῦ Χριστέ, ὁ
ζῶν καὶ μένων εἰς τοὺς αἰῶνας, ἐξαπόστειλον τὸν λό-
γον σου καὶ τὸ πνεῦμα τὸ ἅγιόν σου ἐπὶ τὸν τόπον τοῦ-
10 τον, καὶ ἄνοιξον ἡμῖν τὸν κεκρυμμένον θησαυρὸν τοῦ
ὕδατος εἰς ζωὴν καὶ ἀπόλαυσιν τῶν σῶν πλασμάτων,
ἵνα, ὡς ἐν πᾶσι τοῖς ἁγίοις δοξάζεται τὸ πανάγιον καὶ
φρικτὸν ὄνομά σου, καὶ ἐν ἐμοὶ τῷ ἁμαρτωλῷ δοξασθῇ
σου τὸ μεγαλοπρεπὲς ὄνομα τοῦ πατρὸς καὶ τοῦ υἱοῦ
15 καὶ τοῦ ἁγίου πνεύματος εἰς τοὺς αἰῶνας· ἀμήν.' τελειώσαντος δὲ αὐτοῦ τὴν εὐχὴν καὶ πάντων ἐπακουσάντων
τὸ 'ἀμήν,' ἐδίσταζον οἱ ἄνδρες λέγοντες· 'Ἆρα μὴ ἐν
τούτῳ τῷ τόπῳ μᾶλλον ἢ ἐκείνῳ εὑρήσομεν τὸ ὕδωρ;'
ὁ δὲ δοῦλος τοῦ θεοῦ Νικόλαος λέγει· 'Ἐν τῷ τόπῳ
20 τούτῳ, ἐν ᾧ ἔκλινα τὸ γόνυ, ἐν αὐτῷ ἀπεκάλυψέν μοι
ὁ θεὸς τὴν εὐλογίαν τοῦ ὕδατος.' καὶ λαβὼν δίκελλαν
21Α ὤρυξεν ὀλίγον, καὶ ἐπέδωκεν τὴν δίκελλαν ἑνὶ τῶν παρε-
στώτων κληρικῶν, εἰπών· 'Ὧδε ἐστὶν ἡ εὐλογία, κάμε-
τε.' καὶ ὤρυξαν βάθος τῆς γῆς ὡσεὶ *πῆχυν ἕνα ἥμισυ.*
25 καὶ ἐν αὐτῇ τῇ ὥρᾳ ἔβρυσεν ἡ εὐλογία τοῦ ὕδατος. καὶ
πάντες ἐδόξασαν τὸν θεόν, ὅτι διὰ τῆς εὐχῆς τοῦ δούλου τοῦ θεοῦ Νικολάου ἐφανερώθη ἡ ζωὴ τοῦ ὕδατος,
καὶ προσπεσόντες τοῖς ἴχνεσιν αὐτοῦ παρεκάλεσαν εὔχεσθαι ὑπὲρ αὐτῶν. καὶ πάντες ἐδόξασαν τὸν θεόν, τὸν
30 δώσαντα τὴν ἀποκάλυψιν τῆς ἀληθείας τῷ δούλῳ αὐτοῦ
Νικολάῳ.

24. So they all went out with the servant of God Nicholas, and reached the spot called Kaisar. When the servant of God saw the place, he said to them: "Have faith in God, and let us toil a little, and the Lord God will fulfil your request." And the saint stood on the spot and knelt and prayed to God, saying: "My Master, Lord Jesus Christ, Who livest and abidest forever, send down Thy word and Thy Holy Spirit to this spot, and open for us the hidden treasure of water for the life and enjoyment of Thy creatures, so that, as Thy all-holy and awe-inspiring name is glorified in all the saints, so also in me, the sinner, may be glorified Thy exalted name, of the Father and the Son and of the Holy Spirit, for ever and ever. Amen." When he had finished the prayer, and everyone had heard the Amen, the men doubted, saying: "Will we find the water in this place, rather than in another?" The servant of God Nicholas said: "On this very spot on which I knelt, did God reveal to me the blessing of water." And taking a hoe, he dug a little, and then gave the hoe to one of the clerics standing nearby, saying: "Here is the blessing, go to work." And they dug in the earth, to the depth of one and one half cubits. And at that moment the blessing of the water burst forth. And they all glorified God, that through the prayer of the servant of God Nicholas, the running water had been revealed, and they fell down at his feet and besought him to pray for them. And they all glorified God, who gave the revelation of truth to His servant Nicholas.

ΒΙΟΣ ΤΟΥ ΑΓΙΟΥ ΝΙΚΟΛΑΟΥ

25. Μιᾷ δὲ τῶν ἡμερῶν συνηγμένων τῶν κληρικῶν ἐν
τῇ ἐνδόξῳ ἐκκλησίᾳ τῆς ἁγίας Σιών, λέγουσιν οἱ
κληρικοὶ τῷ δούλῳ τοῦ θεοῦ Νικολάῳ· 'Σήμερον θέλομεν εὐλογηθῆναι καὶ εὐφρανθῆναι παρὰ σοῦ.' ὁ δὲ ἀπε-
5 κρίθη αὐτοῖς λέγων· 'Τὸ θέλημα τοῦ θεοῦ γενέσθω.' καὶ
μετὰ τὴν ἀπόλυσιν τῆς ἁγίας ἐκκλησίας εἰσῆλθον οἱ κληρικοὶ εἰς τὰ ἀκούβιτα τοῦ εὐφραντηρίου, ἵνα ἀριστήσω-
σιν. ὁ δὲ δοῦλος τοῦ θεοῦ, ἰδὼν τοὺς κληρικοὺς καθημέ-
νους εἰς τὰ ἀκούβιτα, εἰσῆλθεν ἐν τῷ κελλαρίῳ καὶ ἐπῆ-
10 ρεν τρεῖς εὐλογίας καὶ ἀρκιόλιον τρίξεστον οἴνου, καὶ
εὐλογήσας ἔδωκεν τῷ δευτεραρίῳ αὐτοῦ λέγων· '῞Υπα-
γε, παράθου αὐτὰ τοῖς κληρικοῖς, ἵνα εὐφρανθῶσιν σήμερον.' ὁ δὲ δευτεράριος ἐποίησεν τὴν ὑπακοὴν τοῦ ἁγίου,
καὶ ἀπελθὼν παρέθηκεν αὐτὰ εἰς τὰ ἀκούβιτα, τὰς τρεῖς
22A15 εὐλογίας καὶ τὸ ἀρκιόλιον. ἰδόντες δὲ οἱ κληρικοὶ τὸ ἀρκιόλιον ὡσεὶ τρίξεστον, κατεγόγγυσαν λέγοντες ὅτι·
'Πρὸς διάκλυσμα ἐν αὐτῷ οὐκ ἔχομεν εὑρεῖν.' γνοὺς δὲ
ὁ δοῦλος τοῦ θεοῦ Νικόλαος τὸν γογγυσμὸν τοῦ κλήρου,
ἀπῆλθεν πρὸς αὐτοὺς λέγων· 'Δεῖ με σήμερον, τεκνία,
20 κεράσαι ὑμῖν.' Καὶ ἦρεν τὸ ἀρκιόλιον ἀπὸ τοῦ τραπεζίου,
καὶ ἐξήτησεν τρία ποτήρια δοθῆναι αὐτῷ, καὶ ἐκέρασεν
πᾶσιν, ὅσον ἤθελον, καὶ εὐφράνθησαν. μετὰ δὲ τὸ εὐφρανθῆναι λέγουσιν οἱ κληρικοὶ εἰς ἑαυτούς· 'Δόξα τῷ
θεῷ τῷ δώσαντι τὴν τοιαύτην χάριν τῷ δούλῳ τοῦ θεοῦ
25 Νικολάῳ. μή τις αὐτῷ ἀπιστήσῃ ἀπὸ τῆς σήμερον
ἡμέρας. πολλὰ γὰρ σημεῖα καὶ θαυμάσια ποιεῖ ὁ θεὸς
δι' αὐτοῦ.'

26. Μιᾷ δὲ τῶν ἡμερῶν ἔρχονται ἄνθρωποι τρεῖς ἀπὸ
τοῦ Πρεσβαίου, τῆς χώρας τῆς καλουμένης 'Ανδρονί-
κου, φέροντες ἄνθρωπον δεδεμένον, ὀνόματι Νικόλαον,
ὃς εἶχεν πνεῦμα ἀκάθαρτον. καὶ λέγουσιν τῷ δούλῳ τοῦ
5 θεοῦ Νικολάῳ ὅτι· 'Πολλὰς ἡμῖν ἐνεδείξατο χειμασίας

48

25. One day, the clerics gathered in the glorious Church of Holy Sion, and the clerics said to the servant of God Nicholas: "Today we wish to receive a blessing from you and to make merry." He answered them, saying: "The wish of God be done." And after the dismissal of the holy congregation, the clerics came to the benches in the refectory to have a meal. When the servant of God Nicholas saw the clerics reclining on the benches, he went to the storeroom, and took three blessed loaves and a small pitcher containing three pints of wine, and blessed them, and gave them to his *deuterarios* saying: "Go and serve these to the clerics, so that they make merry today." The *deuterarios* did the bidding of the saint, and went out and served these things at the benches, the three blessed loaves and the pitcher. When the clerics saw that the pitcher held about three pints, they grumbled, saying: "We will not find in it enough to rinse our mouths." When the servant of God Nicholas became aware of the grumbling of the clergy, he went out to them, saying: "Today, my children, it is my turn to pour for you." And he took the pitcher from the table, and requested that three cups be given to him, and he poured for everyone, as much as they wished, and they made merry. When they had made merry, the clerics said to each other: "Glory be to God, who gave such grace to the servant of God Nicholas. Let no one disbelieve him from this day on. For God does many signs and miracles through him."

26. One day three men came from Presbaion in the district called Andronikos, with a man in fetters by the name of Nicholas, who was possesed by an unclean spirit. And they said to the servant of God Nicholas: "The Devil visited many afflictions upon us, so that we have brought him to

ὁ δαίμων, ἵνα ἐνέγκωμεν αὐτὸν πρὸς τὴν σὴν ἁγιωσύνην.' καὶ λέγει αὐτοῖς ὁ δοῦλος τοῦ θεοῦ Νικόλαος· 'Λύ-
σατε τὸ πλάσμα τοῦ θεοῦ, καὶ ὁ κύριός μου Ἰησοῦς Χριστὸς βοηθῆσαι ἔχει.' τότε οἱ ἄνδρες λέγουσιν τῷ δού-
10 λῳ τοῦ θεοῦ· 'Μή, κύριε· ἴδε, ἀποφυγεῖν ἔχει, καὶ οὐδείς
σου αὐτὸν ἔχει εὑρεῖν.' λέγει δὲ πρὸς αὐτοὺς ὁ δοῦλος
τοῦ θεοῦ Νικόλαος· ''Ο κύριος μακρὰς χεῖρας ἔχει, καὶ
πιάσαι ἔχει αὐτόν.' καὶ ἐπῆρεν ἔλαιον ἐκ τῆς κανδήλας
23A καὶ ἐσφράγισεν αὐτόν, καὶ στὰς ἐπηύξατο αὐτῷ καὶ ἔλυ-
15 σεν αὐτόν. καὶ θελήματι θεοῦ καὶ ταῖς εὐχαῖς τοῦ ὁσίου
μετ' ὀλίγας ἡμέρας ἐξῆλθεν ἀπ' αὐτοῦ τὸ δαιμόνιον. καὶ
ἐγένετο ἔχων ἐν ἑαυτῷ τὸν νοῦν σωφρόνως, καὶ ἀπῆλθεν
εἰς τὸν οἶκον αὐτοῦ δοξάζων καὶ εὐχαριστῶν τῷ θεῷ καὶ
τῷ δούλῳ τοῦ θεοῦ Νικολάῳ.

27. Βουλήσει δὲ τοῦ θεοῦ δευτέρα εἴσοδος ἐγένετο τοῦ
ἀββᾶ Νικολάου ἐν τῇ ἁγίᾳ πόλει Ἰερουσαλήμ, τοῦ προσκυνῆσαι τὸ τίμιον ξύλον τοῦ σταυροῦ καὶ τοὺς ἁγίους
τόπους πάντας καὶ τοὺς τιμίους πατέρας. καὶ πε-
5 ριεργασάμενοι οἱ ὑπηρέται αὐτοῦ ηὗρον πλοῖον ἐν τῷ
Τριστόμῳ Αἰγύπτιον, μέλλοντα πλέειν ἐπὶ Ἀσκάλωνα.
καὶ λέγουσιν τῷ δούλῳ τοῦ θεοῦ Νικολάῳ· 'Κατὰ τὴν
ἐπιθυμίαν τῆς ψυχῆς σου ὁ ἄγγελός σου εὐτρέπισεν
πλοῖον Αἰγύπτιον μέλλοντα πλέειν ἐπὶ Ἀσκάλωνα.' καὶ
10 λέγει ὁ δοῦλος τοῦ θεοῦ Νικόλαος· ''Ο κύριος μακρὰς
χεῖρας ἔχει, καὶ εἴ τι θέλει, παρέχει τοῖς ἀγαπῶσιν
αὐτόν.' καὶ στὰς προσηύξατο ἐπὶ ὥραν ἱκανήν, καὶ μετὰ
τὸ πληρῶσαι τὴν εὐχὴν ἐπακούουσιν αὐτῷ τὸ 'ἀμήν.'
καὶ ἐπῆρεν τῶν ὑπηρετῶν αὐτοῦ δύο, καὶ εἰς αὐτὴν τὴν
24A 15 ἡμέραν τῆς μεσοπεντηκοστῆς * * * τῇ οὖν ἐπαύριον εἰσήλθομεν εἰς τὸ πλοῖον. καὶ δέχονται ἡμᾶς οἱ ναῦται μετὰ
χαρᾶς, καὶ ἔδωκεν ἡμῖν ὁ κύριος ἄνεμον ἐπιτήδειον.

Your Holiness." And the servant of God Nicholas said to them: "Untie God's creature, and my Lord Jesus Christ will help." Then the men said to the servant of God: "O, no, Lord. See, he will run away, and no one will be able to find him." The servant of God Nicholas said to them: "The Lord hath a long arm, and He will lay hold of him." And he took oil from the lamp and made the sign of the cross over him, and stood and prayed over him, and released him. And by the will of God and the prayers of the saint, after a few days the Devil went out of him. And he recovered his senses, and went off to his house glorifying and thanking God and the servant of God Nicholas.

27. By God's will, Father Nicholas made a second journey to the Holy City of Jerusalem, to adore the venerable wood of the Cross and all the Holy Places and the venerable fathers. And his attendants busied themselves and found an Egyptian ship at Tristomon, which was about to sail for Askalon. And they said to the servant of God Nicholas: "In accordance with the desire of your soul, your [guardian] angel has made ready an Egyptian ship, about to sail for Askalon." And the servant of God Nicholas said: "The Lord hath a long arm, and He provides whatever He wishes for those who love him." And he stood and prayed for a long time, and when the prayer was over, they responded to him with the "Amen." And he took two of his attendants, and on the very day of Mid-pentecost * * * and the day after we boarded the ship. And the sailors received us with joy and the Lord gave us a favorable wind.

51

28. Καὶ ὅτε ἐμεσοπελαγοῦμεν, λέγει ὁ δοῦλος τοῦ θεοῦ Νικόλαος· 'Εὔχεσθε πάντες, τέκνα, ὅτι μεγάλη ὀργὴ ἔρχεται πρὸς ἡμᾶς, καὶ μέλλομεν κινδυνεύειν ἐν τῇ θαλάσσῃ.' τότε οἱ ὑπηρέται αὐτοῦ προσέπεσαν τοῖς ποσὶν
5 αὐτοῦ, λέγοντες αὐτῷ· 'Πάτερ, σοὶ μᾶλλον ἐπακούει ὁ θεός· εὖξαι ὑπὲρ ἡμῶν.' καὶ ἀκούσαντες οἱ ναῦται τὰ ῥήματα τοῦ ὁσίου Νικολάου, προσέπεσαν πάντες εἰς τοὺς πόδας αὐτοῦ, μετὰ κλαυθμοῦ λέγοντες· 'Πάτερ, τίς σοι ἀνήγγειλεν, ὅτι ἐπίκειται ἡμῖν ὀργὴ καὶ ὅτι ἀπολ-
10 λύμεθα;' ὁ δὲ δοῦλος τοῦ θεοῦ Νικόλαος λέγει αὐτοῖς· 'Τεκνία μου, εἶδον τὸν διάβολον περικυκλοῦντα τὸ πλοῖον καὶ θέλοντα ἡμᾶς ἐμποδίσαι τῆς εὐθείας ὁδοῦ. οὗτος γὰρ παρέστη τῷ πλοίῳ ἔχων μάχαιραν δίστομον, ὥστε κατασπάσαι ὅλα τὰ σχοινία τὰ ὑπηρετοῦντα τῷ
15 πλοίῳ καὶ βαλεῖν ἡμᾶς ἔξω εἰς τὸ πέλαγος, ἵνα ἀπολώμεθα.' ἦν δὲ ἡμέρα παρασκευή, ὥρα ἐννάτη, ὅτε ταῦτα ἔλεγεν ὁ δοῦλος τοῦ θεοῦ Νικόλαος.

25A **29.** Καὶ στὰς περὶ τὴν δωδεκάτην ὥραν, μετὰ κλαυθμοῦ πικροῦ προσηύξατο πρὸς κύριον λέγων· 'Κύριε Ἰησοῦ Χριστέ, ἐπίφανον τὸ πρόσωπόν σου ἐπὶ πάντας ἡμᾶς καὶ πρόσχες εἰς τὴν θλῖψιν ἡμῶν· καὶ ἐπάκουσον ἡμῶν τῶν
5 ἐπὶ σοὶ ἐλπιζόντων, καὶ μὴ καταισχύνῃς ἡμᾶς, ἀλλὰ ποίησον ἔλεος καὶ ἐπισκοπὴν καὶ λιμὴν γενοῦ ἡμῶν τῶν ἁμαρτωλῶν, ὅτι ἐπτωχεύσαμεν σφόδρα. ταχὺ προκαταλαβέτωσαν ἡμᾶς οἱ οἰκτιρμοί σου, κύριε· δὸς ἡμῖν νίκην κατὰ τοῦ ἀντιπάλου καὶ μισοκάλου διαβόλου· ὅτι
10 εἶδον, πῶς ἐπεισέρχεται πρὸς ἡμᾶς, πειράσαι ἡμᾶς καὶ σαθρῶσαι τὴν πίστιν ἡμῶν. ἀλλὰ πρόφθασον, κύριε Ἰησοῦ Χριστέ, καὶ σβέσον τὰ κέντρα αὐτοῦ, καὶ δὸς ἡμῖν δύναμιν καὶ ἰσχύν, ἵνα καταπατήσωμεν αὐτὸν καὶ δοξάσωμέν σου τὸ ὄνομα εἰς τοὺς αἰῶνας τῶν αἰώνων·
15 ἀμήν.' καὶ μετὰ τὸ πληρῶσαι τὴν εὐχὴν πάντες ὑπήκουσαν τὸ 'ἀμήν.'

28. And when we were in mid-sea, the servant of God Nicholas said: "Pray, all of you, children, for great wrath is coming upon us and we are about to face danger at sea." Then his attendants fell at his feet, saying to him: "Father, God listens rather to you. You pray for us." And when the sailors heard the words of holy Nicholas, they all fell at his feet, wailing and saying: "Father, who made it known to you that wrath is approaching us, and that we are about to perish?" The servant of God Nicholas said to them: "My children, I saw the Devil circling the ship; he is about to throw us off our straight course. For he is present at the ship with a two-edged knife in such a way as to bring down all the rigging which holds the ship together and to hurl us out into the deep, that we may perish." The day was Friday, at the ninth hour, when the servant of God Nicholas spoke these things.

29. And he rose around the twelfth hour and with bitter wailing he prayed to the Lord, saying: "Lord Jesus Christ, let Thy face shine on all of us and give heed to our distress. And hear us who hope in Thee; do not put us to shame, but show us mercy and take care of us, and be a haven unto us sinners, for we have been brought very low. Let Thy tender mercies speedily go before us. O Lord, give us victory against the adversary, that despiser of the good, the Devil, for I saw how he is coming upon us to tempt us and to corrupt our faith. But do Thou come ahead [of him], Lord Jesus Christ and blunt his sting, and give us the power and the strength, that we may trample upon him and glorify Thy name for ever and ever. Amen." And when the prayer was over, they all responded with the "Amen."

30. Καὶ τῇ νυκτὶ ἐκείνῃ ἐγένετο χειμὼν μέγας ἐν τῇ θαλάσσῃ, καὶ ἔμελλεν τὸ πλοῖον καλύπτεσθαι ὑπὸ τῶν κυμάτων. ἰδόντες δὲ οἱ ναῦται ὅτι κινδυνεύουσιν, προσέπεσαν τῷ δούλῳ τοῦ θεοῦ, παρακαλοῦντες καὶ λέγοντες
5 αὐτῷ· 'Κύρι ἀββᾶ, στῆθι καὶ εὖξαι ὑπὲρ ἡμῶν, ὅτι κινδυνεύομεν. καὶ γὰρ ὁ ἄνεμος καὶ τὰ κύματα ἐναντία ἡμῶν εἰσιν.' καὶ λέγει ὁ δοῦλος τοῦ θεοῦ Νικόλαος· "Ὁ κύριος μακρὰς χεῖρας ἔχει καὶ αὐτῷ μελήσει ὑπὲρ τῶν δούλων αὐτοῦ. μόνον πιστεύσωμεν αὐτῷ, ὅτι ἐὰν θέλῃ
26Α10 ὁ θεός, δύναται ἡμᾶς σῶσαι.' καὶ πάλιν κλίνας τὰ γόνατα ὁ δοῦλος τοῦ θεοῦ Νικόλαος ηὔξατο ἐπὶ ὥρας ἱκανάς. καὶ μετὰ τὸ πληρῶσαι τὴν εὐχὴν πάντες ὑπήκουσαν αὐτῷ τὸ 'ἀμήν.' καὶ κατέπαυσεν ὁ ἄνεμος καὶ τὰ κύματα, καὶ γίνεται γαλήνη μεγάλη ἐν τῇ θαλάσσῃ.

31. Ἀπὸ δὲ τῆς χειμασίας τοῦ ἀνέμου ἐξηλώθη τὸ σταυρίον τοῦ καταρτίου καὶ ἐκρέμετο ἐν τῷ ξύλῳ ἄνω. ἦν δέ τις νεανίσκος, ὀνόματι Ἀμμώνιος, πάνυ πρᾶος καὶ ὑπήκοος, καὶ ἐφιλεῖτο παρὰ πᾶσιν ὁ νεανίσκος. ἐξήλω-
5 σεν δὲ αὐτὸν ὁ ἀλλότριος καὶ ἐτήρει πῶς ἀπολέσῃ αὐτόν. αἱ δὲ εὐχαὶ τοῦ μακαρίου ἀββᾶ Νικολάου ἐπρέσβευον πρὸς τὸν κύριον ἡμῶν Ἰησοῦν Χριστόν. τῇ δὲ ἐπαύριον, ἰδὼν ὁ νεανίσκος τὸ σταυρίον ἄνω εἰς τὸ ξύλον κρεμάμενον, ἀναβαίνει ἄνω εἰς τὸ κατάρτιον. καὶ πήξας τὸν
10 σταυρόν, ζηλώσας αὐτὸν ὁ διάβολος ῥίπτει τὸν νεανίσκον ἄνωθεν κάτω, καὶ ἔρχεται εἰς τὸ κραββάτιον, ὅπου ἔκειτο καὶ ἡσύχαζεν ὁ δοῦλος τοῦ θεοῦ Νικόλαος· καὶ ἦν ὡσεὶ νεκρὸς ἄφωνος. καὶ περιεκύκλωσαν αὐτὸν οἱ ναῦται κλαίοντες καὶ ὀλολύζοντες ὅτι· "Ἀπέθανεν ὁ
15 ἀδελφὸς Ἀμμώνιος,' ὅτι· "Ἀπέθανεν κακομόριτος.' ὁ δὲ δοῦλος τοῦ θεοῦ Νικόλαος λέγει τοῖς ναύταις· 'Μὴ κλαίετε, ἀλλὰ μᾶλλον παρακαλέσωμεν τὸν δεσπότην

30. And that night a great storm arose at sea, and the ship was about to be engulfed by the waves. When the sailors saw that they were in jeopardy, they fell down before the servant of God, pleading and saying to him: "Lord Father, rise and pray for us, since we are in danger. For the wind and the waves are against us." And the servant of God Nicholas said: "The Lord hath a long arm, and will take care of his servants. Let us but have faith in Him, that if God wishes, He can save us." And bending his knee once again, the servant of God Nicholas prayed for long hours. And at the end of the prayer they all responded to him with the "Amen." And the wind and the waves stilled, and there was a great calm at sea.

31. The spar of the mast had come unfastened by the fierceness of the wind and hung up there from the beam. There was a certain young man, Ammonios by name, who was very gentle and obedient, and this young man was loved by everyone. But the Alien was envious of him, and kept an eye out for means of destroying him. But the prayers of the blessed Father Nicholas were interceding with our Lord Jesus Christ. The next day, when the youth saw the spar hanging high up from the beam, he climbed up the mast. And when he had fixed the spar fast, the Devil, who was envious of him, threw the youth down from on high, and he landed on the couch where the servant of God Nicholas lay resting; and he was like unto a silent corpse. And the sailors stood around him weeping and wailing: "Our mate Ammonios is dead; the unfortunate one has died!" The servant of God Nicholas said to the sailors: "Weep not, but rather let us beseech God our Master. My

27A θεόν· καὶ ἔχει ὁ κύριός μου Ἰησοῦς Χριστὸς ἐγεῖραι
αὐτόν, κἂν ἀπέθανεν.' ὁ δὲ μακάριος τοῦ θεοῦ δοῦλος
20 Νικόλαος, ἐγγίσας τῷ συντετριμμένῳ νεκρῷ, ἐπηύξατο
αὐτῷ, καὶ σφραγίσας αὐτὸν λέγει τοῖς ναύταις· ῾Ησυ-
χάσατε· ἐλπίζω γὰρ τῷ κυρίῳ μου Ἰησοῦ Χριστῷ, ὅτι
ἐγερεῖ αὐτὸν καὶ πορεύεται μεθ᾽ ἡμῶν εἰς Αἴγυπτον.' ἦν
γὰρ Αἰγύπτιος ὁ πάλιξ. *καὶ προσελθὼν ὁ δοῦλος τοῦ θεοῦ*
25 *τῷ πτώματι καὶ ἐπευξάμενος καὶ κρατήσας αὐτὸν τῆς*
χειρὸς ἤγειρε, λέγων· Λάβετε τὸν ἀδελφὸν ὑμῶν ὑγιαί-
νοντα καὶ μὴ λυπεῖσθε.' οἱ δὲ ἰδόντες τὸ παράδοξον ἐκεῖνο
θαῦμα ἐδόξασαν τὸν θεὸν καὶ τὸν ἅγιον Νικόλαον.

32. Καὶ τῇ ἐπαύριον ἡμέρᾳ ἐφθάσαμεν ἀναφανέντες τὰ
στόμια τῆς Αἰγύπτου. καὶ ὥρμησεν τὸ πλοῖον παρὰ τὸν
αἰγιαλὸν τῆς Αἰγύπτου. λέγουσιν οἱ ναῦται τῷ δούλῳ τοῦ
θεοῦ Νικολάῳ· ᾽Κέλευσον, κύρι ἀββᾶ, εἰσέλθωμεν εἰς
5 τὸν κάραβον καὶ ἀπέλθωμεν εἰς τὴν γῆν τῆς Αἰγύπτου,
εἰς κώμην καλουμένην Διόλκω. καὶ ἔχεις προσκυνῆσαι
τοὺς ἁγίους πάντας καὶ τοὺς οἴκους ἡμῶν εὐλογῆσαι,
ὅτι ὁ θεὸς ἔδωκέν σοι δύναμιν, καὶ χάριν εὗρες παρ᾽
αὐτῷ. τὸν γὰρ ἀδελφὸν Ἀμμώνιον διὰ τῶν εὐχῶν σου
10 ἀνέστησεν ὁ θεός, καὶ ἔχει ἐλθεῖν μεθ᾽ ἡμῶν, ὅτι καὶ ἡ
χώρα αὐτοῦ ὧδε ἐστὶν εἰς Αἴγυπτον.' λέγει δὲ ὁ δοῦλος
τοῦ θεοῦ Νικόλαος· ᾽Εἰ θέλημα τοῦ θεοῦ ἐστιν, ἄγωμεν.'
καὶ εἰσήλθομεν εἰς τὴν κώμην τὴν λεγομένην Διόλκω.
καὶ ἀκοὴ ἐγένετο περὶ τοῦ ἀββᾶ Νικολάου, ὅτι ἄνθρω-
28A 15 πος ἀγαθὸς ὑπάρχει καὶ δοῦλος τοῦ θεοῦ. καὶ ἦλθον εἰς
ἀπάντησιν αὐτοῦ, ἵνα εὐλογηθῶσιν παρ᾽ αὐτοῦ. τότε λέγει ὁ δοῦλος τοῦ θεοῦ Νικόλαος τοῖς ἀπαντήσασιν αὐτῷ·
῾Εγώ, ἀδελφοί, ἄνθρωπός εἰμι ἁμαρτωλός· ἀλλ᾽ ὁ κύριος Ἰησοῦς Χριστὸς εὐλογήσει ὑμᾶς.' καὶ εἰσελθὼν ὁ

Lord Jesus Christ will raise him, even though he be dead.''
The blessed servant of God Nicholas drew near to the
bruised corpse, prayed over it, made the sign of the cross
over it, and said to the sailors: ''Calm down, for I have
hope in my Lord Jesus Christ that He will raise him; and
he will journey with us to Egypt.'' For the lad was an Egyptian. And the servant of God approached the corpse,
prayed over it, took the lad by the hand, and raised him
saying: ''Receive your shipmate safe and sound and grieve
not.'' When they beheld this strange wonder, they glorified
God and Saint Nicholas.

32. And the next day, we arrived in sight of the Egyptian
Delta. And the ship anchored on the shore of Egypt. The
sailors said to the servant of God Nicholas: ''If you please,
Lord Father, let us get in the dinghy and betake ourselves
to the soil of Egypt, to the village called Diolko. And you
shall adore all the saints, and bless our houses, for God
gave you the power and you have found grace with Him.
For God resurrected our shipmate Ammonios through your
prayers, and he will come with us, since his [native] land
is here in Egypt.'' The servant of God Nicholas said: ''If
this be the will of God, let us go.'' And we entered the
village called Diolko. And word went around about Father
Nicholas that he was a good man, and the servant of God.
And they came to meet him, in order to be blessed by him.
Then said the servant of God Nicholas to those who had
come to meet him: ''I, brothers, am a sinful man. But the
Lord Jesus Christ will bless you.'' And the servant of God

20 δοῦλος τοῦ θεοῦ εἰς τὴν κώμην τὴν λεγομένην Διόλκω,
κατέλυσεν εἰς τὴν ἐκκλησίαν τοῦ ἁγίου Θεοδώρου. καὶ
ἦν προσευχόμενος τῷ θεῷ ἀδιαλείπτως κατὰ πᾶσαν
ὥραν, ὅτι ὁ κύριος Ἰησοῦς Χριστὸς ἀνέστησεν τὸν ἄνθρωπον καὶ ἐζωοποίησεν αὐτὸν καὶ ἔστη ἐνώπιον αὐτοῦ
25 ὑγιής. καὶ ἐποίησεν ἐν τῇ ἁγίᾳ ἐκκλησίᾳ τοῦ ἁγίου Θεοδώρου τετάρτην ἡμέραν.

33. Ἦν δέ τις ἄνθρωπος τυφλός, ὀνόματι Ἀντώνιος,
καὶ ἐκάθητο ἐν τῇ ἁγίᾳ ἐκκλησίᾳ, μὴ βλέπων τὸ σύνολον. καὶ ἰδὼν αὐτὸν ὁ δοῦλος τοῦ θεοῦ Νικόλαος λέγει
αὐτῷ· 'Πόσα ἔτη ἔχεις μὴ βλέπων;' καὶ λέγει αὐτῷ ὁ
5 τυφλός· 'Εἰσὶν ἔτη τρία, ἀφ' οὗ τὸν ἥλιον οὐκ εἶδον. καὶ
πολλὰ χρήματα ἐδαπάνησα εἰς τοὺς ἰατρούς, ἵνα ποιή-
σωσίν με ἀναβλέψαι· καὶ οὐδέν μοι ὄφελος ἐγένετο, ἀλλ'
εἰς αὐτοὺς ἐδαπάνησα πάντα τὰ ἐμά.' ὁ δὲ δοῦλος τοῦ
θεοῦ Νικόλαος λέγει αὐτῷ· 'Καὶ διὰ τί οὐκ ἐπίστευσας
10 τοῖς ἁγίοις, καὶ εἶχες θεραπευθῆναι δίχα χρημάτων;' λέγει αὐτῷ ὁ τυφλός· 'Καὶ ὅτι ἄπιστος εὑρήθην, τί ποιήσω;'
λέγει αὐτῷ ὁ δοῦλος τοῦ θεοῦ Νικόλαος· 'Πιστεύεις ἀπὸ
τοῦ νῦν, ὅτι δύνανταί σε οἱ ἅγιοι θεραπεῦσαι;' λέγει αὐτῷ
ὁ τυφλός· 'Πιστεύω τῷ θεῷ καὶ ταῖς ἁγίαις σου εὐχαῖς,
15 ὅτι δύνασαι δυσωπῆσαι τὸν θεόν, ἵνα με ἐλεήσῃ.' σπλαγ-
χνισθεὶς δὲ ὁ δοῦλος τοῦ θεοῦ καὶ στὰς ηὔξατο ἐπ' αὐτῷ·
καὶ ἐπῆρεν ἔλαιον ἐκ τῆς κανδήλας τοῦ ἁγίου Θεοδώρου, καὶ ποιήσας εἰς τοὺς ὀφθαλμοὺς αὐτοῦ τὸ σημεῖον
τοῦ σταυροῦ λέγει αὐτῷ· 'Πιστεύω τῷ θεῷ, ὅτι αὔριον
29Α20 βλέπεις τὴν δόξαν τοῦ θεοῦ ἰδίοις ὀφθαλμοῖς.' καὶ τῇ
αὔριον ἡμέρᾳ ἠνεῴχθησαν οἱ ὀφθαλμοὶ τοῦ τυφλοῦ, καὶ
περιεπάτει βλέπων καὶ ἐδόξαζεν τὸν θεόν, ὅτι διὰ τῆς
εὐχῆς τοῦ δούλου τοῦ θεοῦ ἀνέβλεψεν.

entered the village called Diolko, and took up lodging in the Church of Saint Theodore. And he prayed to God without interruption at all hours, since the Lord Jesus Christ had resurrected the man and brought him back to life, and he stood before him whole. And he spent four days [?][1] in the Church of St. Theodore.

33. There was a blind man, named Anthony, who dwelt in the holy church, unable to see anything at all. And when the servant of God Nicholas saw him, he said to him: "How many years have you been without your sight?" And the blind man said to him: "It is now three years since I saw the sun. And I spent much money on doctors so that they would restore my sight. But it has been all of no avail, though I spent on them all that I had." The servant of God Nicholas said to him: "And why did you not put your faith in the saints? You would have been cured free of charge." And the blind man said to him: "Now that I have been found to be without faith, what should I do?" The servant of God Saint Nicholas said to him: "Will you believe from now on that the saints have the power to cure you?" The blind man said to him: "I put my faith in God and in your holy prayers, that you can persuade God to have mercy on me." Moved with compassion, the servant of God stood praying over him. And he took oil from the lamp of Saint Theodore, and made the sign of the cross upon his eyes, and said to him: "I have faith in God that tomorrow you will see the glory of God with your own eyes." And the following day the eyes of the blind man were opened, and he walked around seeing, and glorified God that he had recovered his sight through the prayer of the servant of God.

[1]Or "Wednesday."

34. Παραχρῆμα δὲ καὶ ἄλλος τις, ἰδὼν ὅτι ἀνέβλεψεν
ὁ τυφλὸς διὰ τῶν εὐχῶν τοῦ ὁσίου Νικολάου, προσέπεσεν τῷ δούλῳ τοῦ θεοῦ λέγων· 'Κύρι ἀββᾶ, ἐγὼ ἔχω τεσ-
σάρεις μῆνας κυλιόμενος εἰς τὸ ἔδαφος, πονῶν μου τὰ
5 ἐντός. καὶ φρικίαι μοί εἰσι τοῦ σώματος, καὶ οὐ δύναμαι καθῖσαι εἰς τὴν ἰδίαν μου χρείαν καὶ ἀπαλλάσσειν
με, καὶ οὐκέτι εἰς βρῶσιν ἔρχομαι, ἀλλ᾽ ἐνεκρώθην, τὴν
κόπρον τῆς κοιλίας μου βαστάζων. καὶ πολλὰ ἐδαπάνησα εἰς τοὺς ἰατρούς, καὶ οὐδέν μοι ὄφελος ἐγένετο, ἀλλ᾽
10 εἰς μάτην ἐδαπάνησα τὰ ἐμὰ πάντα.' καὶ λέγει αὐτῷ ὁ
δοῦλος τοῦ θεοῦ Νικόλαος· ''Εγώ σε προσφέρω ἰατρῷ
τῷ δυναμένῳ σε ἰάσασθαι ἄνευ ἀργυρίου.' λέγει ὁ ἄν-
θρωπος· 'Καὶ τίς ἐστιν, ἵνα με ἐλεήσῃ τάχιον;' καὶ λέγει
ὁ δοῦλος τοῦ θεοῦ Νικόλαος· '῏Ωδε παραστήκει ἡμῖν.'
15 ὁ δὲ ἀσθενῶν ἔβλεπεν ὧδε κἀκεῖ, ἰδεῖν τὸν ἰατρόν, καὶ
λέγει τῷ μακαρίῳ ἀββᾶ· 'Οὐδένα βλέπω, κύρι ἀββᾶ.'
λέγει αὐτῷ ὁ δοῦλος τοῦ θεοῦ· ''Εὰν πιστεύσῃς τῷ ἐμῷ
ἰατρῷ, ἔχω αὐτὸν παρακαλέσαι, ἵνα σε ἰάσηται καὶ ψυχῇ
καὶ σώματι.' λέγει δὲ αὐτῷ ὁ ἄνθρωπος· ''Εγὼ πιστεύω
20 τῷ θεῷ καὶ εἰς τὴν σὴν ἁγιωσύνην.' ὁ δὲ δοῦλος τοῦ θεοῦ
Νικόλαος προσηύξατο, καὶ σφραγίσας αὐτὸν λέγει
αὐτῷ· ''Εν ὀνόματι τοῦ κυρίου μου Ἰησοῦ Χριστοῦ θερα-
πεύθητι ἀπὸ τῆς ὥρας ταύτης.' καὶ πιστεύσας ὁ ἄνθρωπος τῷ θεῷ καὶ τῷ δούλῳ αὐτοῦ Νικολάῳ ἐξ ὅλης καρ-
25 δίας, ἰάθη ἀπὸ τῆς ὥρας ἐκείνης. καὶ ἀπῆλθεν εἰς τὸν
οἶκον αὐτοῦ, δοξάζων τὸν θεόν, ὅτι διὰ τεσσάρων μη-
νῶν ἔφαγεν καὶ ἔπιεν καὶ οὐδὲν αὐτῷ οὐκέτι ἐδυσ-
χέραινεν.

35. Ὁ δὲ δοῦλος τοῦ θεοῦ Νικόλαος ἐξῆλθεν ἀπὸ τῆς
κώμης τῆς λεγομένης Διόλκω, καὶ εἰσῆλθεν εἰς τὸ

34. Right away another man, who had seen that the blind man had regained his sight through the prayers of holy Nicholas, fell before the servant of God saying: "Lord Father, I have been rolling along the ground for four months, suffering in my insides. And I have body tremors, and am unable to sit to do my natural need and to relieve myself; I no longer go to have a meal, but am as good as dead, carrying around the excrement of my belly. And I spent much on doctors, and it has been all of no avail, but I spent all that I had in vain." And the servant of God Nicholas said to him: "I am going to take you to a doctor who can cure you free of charge." The man said: "And who is he, that he may have pity on me right away?" And the servant of God Nicholas said: "He is here right among us." And the sick man looked around right and left to find the doctor, and said to the blessed father: "I don't see anyone, Lord Father." The servant of God said to him: "If you have faith in my doctor, I will beseech Him to cure you in soul as well as in body." The man said to him: "I have faith in God and in Your Holiness." The servant of God Nicholas prayed and made the sign of the cross over him, and said to him: "In the name of my Lord Jesus Christ, be cured from this moment on." And the man believed with all his heart in God, and in His servant Nicholas, and he was cured from then on. And he went off to his house, praising God, for after four months he [was able] to eat and drink and he no longer felt any discomfort.

35. The servant of God Nicholas left the village called Diolko, and he boarded the ship, and went by sea to

30A πλοῖον, καὶ πλεύσας ἦλθεν εἰς Ἀσκάλωνα. καὶ ἀνῆλθεν
εἰς τὴν ἁγίαν πόλιν ἐν ἡμέρᾳ δευτέρᾳ, καὶ εἰσῆλθεν εἰς
5 τὴν ἁγίαν Ἀνάστασιν τοῦ Χριστοῦ, καὶ ηὔξατο εἰς τὸν
ἅγιον Γολγοθᾶ προσκυνήσας. καὶ ὅτε ἔφθασεν ἐν ᾧ ἔκειτο τὸ πεποθημένον ξύλον τοῦ τιμίου σταυροῦ, θελήματι
τοῦ θεοῦ ἠνεῴχθησαν αἱ θύραι τοῦ ναοῦ καὶ ἐδέξαντο
τὸν δοῦλον τοῦ θεοῦ Νικόλαον, καὶ προσεκύνησεν τὸν
10 τίμιον σταυρὸν ἐν ἡμέρᾳ δευτέρᾳ. καὶ ἐποίησεν ἐν τῇ
ἁγίᾳ πόλει προσκυνῶν τοὺς ἁγίους τόπους πάντας καὶ
τοὺς τιμίους πατέρας ἕως τοῦ Ἰορδάνου ἡμέρας ὀκτὼ
διατρίψας. καὶ παρέστη αὐτῷ ἄγγελος κυρίου λέγων·
'Σπούδασον, βάδιζε εἰς τὴν Λυκίαν, τὴν χώραν σου.'

36. Καὶ ἐξελθὼν κατέβη εἰς Ἀσκάλωνα, καὶ ηὗρεν
πλοῖον Ῥόδιον· *ἦν γὰρ* εὐτρεπισμένον *τὸ πλοῖον* ὑπὸ τοῦ
ἀγγέλου τοῦ ὀφθέντος αὐτῷ ἐν τῇ ἁγίᾳ πόλει καὶ εἰπόν-
τος· 'Σπούδασον εἰς τὴν Λυκίαν.' καὶ λέγει ὁ δοῦλος
5 τοῦ θεοῦ τῷ ναυκλήρῳ· '"Οντως, κύρι ναύκληρε, ποῦ
πορεύει;' καὶ λέγει αὐτῷ ὁ ναύκληρος· 'Ἐὰν θέλῃ ὁ θεός,
εἰς Κωνσταντίνου *πόλιν* θέλομεν. ἀλλὰ πρὸ τριῶν ἡμερῶν ἠθέλομεν, καὶ ἐμποδιζόμεθα ἐν τῇ πόλει ταύτῃ, καὶ
ἐξερχόμενοι τοῦ ἀναχωρῆσαι, τὸν αὐτὸν ἐμποδισμὸν
10 πανθάνομεν. λοιπὸν οὐκ οἴδαμεν, τίς ἐστιν ἐν ἡμῖν ἐμπό-
διος· ὅλα γὰρ τὰ πλοῖα ἔπλευσαν, καὶ ἡμεῖς ὧδέ ἐσμεν.'
καὶ λέγει ὁ δοῦλος τοῦ θεοῦ Νικόλαος· 'Λάβετέ με εἰς
τὸ πλοῖον ὑμῶν, καὶ ὁ κύριος βοηθήσει ὑμῖν.' καὶ λέγουσιν αὐτῷ οἱ ναῦται· '"Ανελθε μετὰ χαρᾶς, ἀββᾶ· ἴσως
31A15 ὁ κύριος διὰ τῶν εὐχῶν *ὑμῶν* ἀνεμποδίστους ἡμᾶς ποιή-
σει.' ὁ δὲ δοῦλος τοῦ θεοῦ Νικόλαος ἀνέρχεται εἰς τὸ
πλοῖον, καὶ ποιεῖ εὐχήν, καὶ ἀποπλέουσιν.

Askalon. And he went up to the Holy City on a Monday, .
and went into the Holy Church of Christ's Resurrection,
and he prayed at Holy Golgotha and adored it. And when
he reached [the place] wherein lay the much desired wood
of the Venerable Cross, by the will of God the portals of
the church opened, and received the servant of God
Nicholas, and he adored the Venerable Cross on [that]
Monday. And he spent eight days in the Holy City, ador-
ing all the holy places and the venerable fathers as far away
as the Jordan. And an angel of the Lord [appeared and]
stood by him saying: "Make haste and proceed to Lycia,
to your country."

36. And he left and went down to Askalon, and found a
Rhodian ship, for it had been made ready by the angel who
had appeared to him in the Holy City and had said: "Make
haste for Lycia." And the servant of God said to the skipper: "Truly, skipper, where are you bound?" And the skipper said to him: "God willing, we will [go] to Constantinople. But we were about to sail three days ago, and are
[still] held up in this city, and whenever we set out to sail
back, we encounter the same impediment. So we do not
know who among us is impeding us. For all the ships have
sailed away, but we ourselves are [still] here." And the servant of God Nicholas said: "Take me in your boat, and
the Lord will help you." And the sailors said to him: "You
are welcome on board, Father. Perhaps the Lord will free
us from impediment through your prayers." The servant
of God Nicholas boarded the ship, said a prayer, and they
sailed away.

37. Θελήματι δὲ τοῦ θεοῦ διὰ δέκα ἡμερῶν ἀναβαίνουσιν εἰς Λυκίαν, εἰς τὰ ὄρη Χελιδόνος, ἐγγὺς τοῦ λεγομένου Φοίνικος. καὶ λέγει ὁ δοῦλος τοῦ θεοῦ Νικόλαος τῷ ναυ-κλήρῳ· "Ὧδέ ἐστιν ὁ τόπος ἡμῶν, ἐν ᾧ ἔχομεν ἐξελθεῖν
5 καὶ ἀνελθεῖν εἰς τὸ μοναστήριον ἡμῶν.' οἱ δὲ ναῦται λέ-γουσιν τῷ ἀββᾷ· "Ἐπιτήδειον ἄνεμον ἔχομεν θεοῦ θέ-λοντος, κύρι ἀββᾶ, καὶ οὐ δυνάμεθα παραβαλεῖν ὧδε, ὅπου λέγεις Φοίνικα.' καὶ λέγει αὐτοῖς· 'Κἂν εἰς Ἀνδρι-άκην;' λέγει ὁ ναύκληρος· 'Οὐδὲ εἰς Ἀνδριάκην, οὐδὲ
10 εἰς τὸ Τρίστομον, ἀλλ᾽ εἰς τὴν Ῥόδον.' καὶ λέγει ὁ δοῦ-λος τοῦ θεοῦ· 'Οὐχὶ συνέθου μοι ὧδε παραβαλεῖν, ἵνα ἐξέλθωμεν;' καὶ λέγει ὁ ναύκληρος· 'Ναί, κύρι ἀββᾶ, ἀλλὰ τὸν ἄνεμον τοῦτον σφοδρῶς ἔχει τὸ πλοῖον· καὶ τίς δύναται κρατῆσαι αὐτό, ἵνα σὲ ἐκβάλωμεν ὧδε;' ὁ
15 δὲ δοῦλος τοῦ θεοῦ Νικόλαος σύνδακρυς ἐγένετο, καὶ λέγει πρὸς τοὺς ἀδελφοὺς αὐτοῦ· "Ὥρα ἐστὶν τῆς δω-δεκάτης· δεῦτε, εὐξώμεθα πάντες.' καὶ ηὔξαντο κατὰ τὴν δοθεῖσαν αὐτοῖς πίστιν ὑπὸ τοῦ μεγάλου βασιλέως. καὶ μετὰ τὴν εὐχὴν εἶπεν αὐτοῖς· 'Δεῦτε, λάβωμεν τρο-
20 φῆς τοῦ δείπνου, καὶ μηδὲν μεριμνήσωμεν· ὁ γὰρ ὑμνο-λόγος Δαβὶδ εἶπεν· «ἐπίρριψον ἐπὶ κύριον τὴν μέριμνάν σου, καὶ αὐτός σε διαθρέψει.» δεῦτε οὖν, καὶ ἡμεῖς ἐπιρ-ρίψωμεν τὴν μέριμναν ἡμῶν ἐπὶ κύριον τὸν θεὸν ἡμῶν, καὶ ἔχει ὁ κύριος βοηθῆσαι.' καὶ ἤκουσαν τοῦ ῥή-
25 ματος αὐτοῦ, καὶ ἐδείπνησαν, καὶ μετὰ τὸ δεῖπνον ἔβα-λον εὐχαριστίαν τῷ θεῷ. καὶ λέγει ὁ δοῦλος τοῦ θεοῦ·
32Α "Ὀλίγον ἀνακτησώμεθα ἑαυτοὺς πρὸς ὕπνον καὶ ἀνα-πάωμεν.' ὁ δὲ δοῦλος τοῦ θεοῦ ηὔχετο· 'Κύριε, μὴ θλίψῃς ἡμᾶς εἰς τὸ πέλαγος τοῦτο, ἀλλὰ βοήθησον ἡμῖν.'

37. By the will of God in ten days they sailed up to Lycia, to the Chelidon Mountains, near a place called Phoinix. And the servant of God Nicholas said to the skipper: "Here is our place, where we should disembark and go up to our monastery." The sailors said to the Father: "God willing, we have a favorable wind, Lord Father, and cannot put in here at the place you call Phoinix." And he said to them: "Then at least at Andriake?" The skipper said, "Not at Andriake either, nor at Tristomon, but at Rhodes." And the servant of God said: "Did you not agree with me that you would put in here, so that we could disembark?" And the skipper said: "I did, Lord Father, but the ship holds firmly to this wind. And who can stop it, so that we may put you ashore here?" The servant of God Nicholas broke into tears and said to his brethren: "It is the twelfth hour. Here, let us all pray." And they prayed in accordance with the faith given them by the Great Ruler. And after the prayer, he said to them: "Here, let us partake of supper, and not worry at all. For David, the singer of hymns, said: 'Cast thy care upon the Lord, and He shall sustain thee.' Here, then, let us also cast our care upon the Lord our God, and the Lord will help." And they listened to his words, and they supped, and after the meal they offered thanks to God. And the servant of God said: "Let us restore ourselves with a little sleep; let us rest." The servant of God prayed: "O, Lord, do not afflict us here in this open sea, but help us."

38. Τὸ δὲ πλοῖον ἤμελλεν παρέρχεσθαι τὸ Τρίστομον· καὶ εὐθέως ἐξήγειρεν κύριος ὁ θεὸς ἄνεμον ἀπὸ δυσμῶν, καὶ ἔστρεψεν τὸ πλοῖον καὶ ἐφέρετο ὧδε κἀκεῖσε καὶ ἐκινδύνευεν. ὁ δὲ ναύκληρος διενοήσατο ὅτι· ''Η χειμασία
5 αὕτη οὐκ ἔστιν ἄλλως, εἰ μὴ διὰ τὴν παρακοήν, ἥνπερ ἐποιήσαμεν τῷ δούλῳ τοῦ θεοῦ Νικολάῳ.' καὶ λέγει τοῖς ναύταις· 'Βάλετε τὰ σίδηρα τοῦ πλοίου εἰς τὴν γῆν, καὶ δήσατε τὸ πλοῖον ἡμῶν, καὶ φέρετε τὸν κάραβον· ἄφες ἐξέλθῃ ὁ ἀββᾶς μετὰ τῶν ἀδελφῶν εἰς τὸν τόπον αὐτοῦ.
10 οἶδα γὰρ ὅτι αἱ εὐχαὶ αὐτοῦ μεγάλαι εἰσὶν πρὸς τὸν θεόν· καὶ τοῦτο ἐποίησεν εἰς ἡμᾶς ὁ θεός, ἵνα μὴ λυπηθῇ ὁ ἀββᾶς.' τότε λέγει ὁ ναύκληρος· ''Ελθέ, κύρι ἀββᾶ· κατὰ τὸ ῥῆμά σου ἔξελθε, καὶ ὕπαγε εἰς τὸ μοναστήριόν σου, καὶ εὖξαι ὑπὲρ ἡμῶν, ἵνα ὁ κύριος δώσῃ ἡμῖν διὰ τῶν
15 εὐχῶν σου ἐπιτήδειον ἄνεμον, ἵνα πλεύσωμεν καὶ εὐχαριστήσωμεν τῷ θεῷ διὰ τῶν ὁσίων σου εὐχῶν.' καὶ λέγει ὁ δοῦλος τοῦ θεοῦ Νικόλαος· 'Τὸ θέλημα τοῦ θεοῦ γινέσθω.' καὶ εἰσῆλθεν εἰς τὸν κάραβον καὶ ἦλθεν εἰς ᾿Ανδριάκην. καὶ εὐχαρίστησαν πάντες τῷ θεῷ καὶ τῷ δούλῳ
20 αὐτοῦ Νικολάῳ, ὅτι κατὰ τὸ ῥῆμα, ὃ εἶπεν· «ἐπίρριψον ἐπὶ κύριον τὴν μέριμνάν σου, καὶ αὐτός σε διαθρέψει,» ἐγένετο οὕτως. καὶ ἀνῆλθεν εἰς τὸ μοναστήριον τῆς ἁγίας Σιὼν εἰς τὸ ὄρος. καὶ συνήχθησαν ὄχλοι πολλοὶ εἰς προσκύνησιν τοῦ δούλου τοῦ θεοῦ Νικολάου. καὶ ἦν
25 ἀγαλλίασις καὶ χαρὰ μεγάλη, καὶ πάντες ἐδόξαζον τὸν θεόν.

33A   **39.** Ἐν δὲ ταῖς ἡμέραις ἐκείναις, ὅτε τὸ ὄρος ἐλατομεῖτο ἔμπροσθεν τῆς κόγχης, λέγει ὁ δοῦλος τοῦ θεοῦ Νικόλαος πρὸς τοὺς ἀδελφούς· 'Πόθος μοι ἐγένετο ἀπελθεῖν πρὸς τοὺς ἁγίους τόπους, προσκυνῆσαι τὸν τίμιον

38. The ship was about to pass by Tristomon, when suddenly the Lord God raised a wind from the West, and turned the ship around and tossed it back and forth, and it was in peril. The skipper thought: "This storm can only come from the disobedience we showed toward the servant of God Nicholas." And he said to the sailors: "Throw the ship's anchor to the bottom, and tie up our boat and fetch the dinghy. Let the Father and the brethren get off at this place. For I know that his prayers have great power with God. And God did this to us, so that the Father would not be distressed." Then the skipper said: "Come, Lord Father. Disembark according to your words, go to your monastery, and pray for us, so that by your prayers the Lord may give us a favorable wind and we may sail on and give thanks to God through your holy prayers." And the servant of God Nicholas said: "The will of God be done." And he boarded the dinghy and arrived at Andriake. And they all gave thanks to God and to His servant Nicholas, that it had to come to pass exactly according to the words which he uttered: "Cast thy care upon the Lord, and He shall sustain thee." And he went to the Monastery of Holy Sion up the mountain. And a large crowd gathered in order to adore the servant of God Nicholas. And there was great exultation and joy and everyone praised God.

39. In those days, when the hill in front of the apse was being quarried, the servant of God Nicholas said to the brethren: "I yearn to go off to the Holy Places, to adore

5 σταυρὸν καὶ τὴν ἁγίαν Ἀνάστασιν τοῦ Χριστοῦ· καὶ ἐὰν
μου ἀκούητε, ἀπολύσωμεν τοὺς τεχνίτας τοὺς λιθοτό-
μους.᾽ καὶ λέγει αὐτῷ ὁ ἀδελφὸς αὐτοῦ Ἀρτεμᾶς· ᾽Τί
γάρ; ἡμεῖς οὐ δυνάμεθα ἄρξαι τῶν τεχνιτῶν;᾽ καὶ λέγει
αὐτῷ· ᾽Οὐχί· ἐμοὶ γὰρ ἐχαρίσατο ὁ θεὸς τὴν τοιαύτην
10 χάριν καὶ ὑπακούει μοι ὁ λίθος καὶ ὡς θέλω, ποιῶ.᾽ καὶ
λέγουσιν αὐτῷ· ᾽Οὓς θέλεις, ἀπόλυσον.᾽ καὶ ἀπέλυσεν
αὐτούς. καὶ ἀπελθὼν ὁ δοῦλος τοῦ θεοῦ εἰς τοὺς ἁγίους
τόπους, αὐθεντήσας ὁ ἀδελφὸς αὐτοῦ Ἀρτεμᾶς πέμπει
καὶ καλεῖ τοὺς τεχνίτας εἰς Ἀρνέας, καὶ ἐλθόντες πρὸς
15 τὸ ὄρος λατομοῦσιν. καὶ ἠθέλησαν στρέψαι ἕνα λίθον.
καὶ πέμπει ὁ ἀδελφὸς αὐτοῦ Ἀρτεμᾶς εἰς ὅλην τὴν κώμην, καὶ συνήγαγεν ἀνθρώπους ὡς ἑβδομήκοντα πέντε
τὸν ἀριθμόν, χωρὶς τῶν τεχνιτῶν. καὶ ὅλην τὴν ἡμέραν
πυκτεύσαντες ἑνὶ λίθῳ οὐκ ἴσχυσαν στρέψαι αὐτόν, ἵνα
20 πληρωθῇ ὁ λόγος τοῦ δούλου τοῦ θεοῦ, ὃν εἶπεν· ᾽Οὐχί,᾽
ὅτι χωρὶς αὐτοῦ οὐκ ἐστράφη εἷς λίθος. καὶ μετὰ τὸ ἐλθεῖν τὸν δοῦλον τοῦ θεοῦ Νικόλαον ἀπὸ τῶν τόπων τῶν
ἁγίων, ἐκάλεσεν δώδεκα ὀνόματα τῶν ἀδελφῶν, καὶ
ἀπελθὼν ἔστρεψεν τὸν λίθον. καὶ ἐδόξασαν τὸν θεὸν
25 πάντες οἱ *ἰδόντες καὶ* ἀκούσαντες, ὅτι δύναμις κυρίου
ἦν ἐπ᾽ αὐτόν, καὶ οὐ μόνον οἱ ἄνθρωποι, ἀλλὰ καὶ οἱ
λίθοι ὑπακούουσιν αὐτῷ.

40. Πάλιν ἐν μιᾷ τῶν ἡμερῶν ἔρχεται ἀνδρόγυνον ἀπὸ
Ζηνουπόλεως εἰς τὸ μοναστήριον, καὶ προσπίπτουσιν
εἰς τοὺς πόδας τοῦ δούλου τοῦ θεοῦ Νικολάου, καὶ λέ-
34Α γουσιν αὐτῷ· ᾽Ἐλέησον ἡμᾶς, δοῦλε τοῦ θεοῦ, ὅτι τριά-
5 κοντα ἔτη ἔχομεν, ἐξ ὅτου τὸν γάμον ἐποιήσαμεν, καὶ
παιδίον οὐκ ἔσχαμεν. καὶ ἠκούσαμεν περὶ τῆς ὁσίας
ὑμῶν εὐχῆς, καὶ ἤλθαμεν *παρακαλέσαι* τὸν θεὸν καὶ τὴν
ἁγιωσύνην ὑμῶν. καὶ εὖξη ὑπὲρ ἡμῶν, ἵνα σπλαγχνισθῇ

the Venerable Cross and the Holy [Church of the] Resurrection of Christ. And if you agree, let us dismiss the craftsmen, the stone-masons.'' And his brother Artemas said to him, ''How so? Can't *I* direct the craftsmen?'' And he said to him, ''No! God granted me this grace, the stone obeys me, and I do as I wish.'' And they said to him: ''Dismiss whomever you wish.'' And he dismissed them. And while the servant of God was gone to the Holy Places, his brother Artemas had usurped authority; he sent for and summoned the craftsmen to Arneai, and they came to the mountain and began to quarry. And they wanted to turn over a block. And his brother Artemas sent [word] throughout the village, and collected men, around seventy-five in number, not counting the craftsmen. And all day long they struggled with that block, but they could not turn it over, so that the word of the servant of God might be fulfilled, when he said: ''No!'' since not a single block was turned in his absence. And after the servant of God returned from the Holy Places, he summoned twelve people from among the brethren, and went [with them] and turned the block over. And God was praised by all those who had seen and heard that the power of the Lord was upon him, and that not only men obeyed him, but stones as well.

40. Again, one day a couple came from Zenoupolis to the monastery. And they fell at the feet of the servant of God Nicholas, and said to him: ''Have mercy on us, servant of God, for thirty years have passed since we were married, and we have produced no child. And we heard about your holy prayer and we came to entreat God and Your Holiness. And pray for us, so that God will be moved with

ὁ θεὸς ἐφ᾽ ἡμᾶς καὶ δώῃ ἡμῖν καρπόν.᾽ καὶ λέγει αὐτοῖς
10 ὁ δοῦλος τοῦ θεοῦ· ῞Εὰν πιστεύητε ἐξ ὅλης τῆς καρδίας
ὑμῶν εἰς τὸν κύριόν μου ᾽Ιησοῦν Χριστόν, δοῦναι ὑμῖν
ἔχει.᾽ καὶ λέγουσιν αὐτῷ· ῾Πιστεύομεν τῷ θεῷ, ὅτι διὰ
τῆς προσευχῆς σου δύναται ὁ θεὸς δοῦναι ἡμῖν.᾽ καὶ
στὰς προσηύξατο ἐπὶ ὥραν ἱκανήν, καὶ λαβὼν ἔλαιον
15 ἐκ τῆς κανδήλας ἐσφράγισεν αὐτοὺς εἰς τὸ ὄνομα τοῦ
πατρὸς καὶ τοῦ υἱοῦ καὶ τοῦ ἁγίου πνεύματος, καὶ ἀπέλυσεν αὐτούς. καὶ μετὰ τὸν ἐνιαυτὸν ἦλθον μετὰ τέκνου
ἄρρενος. καὶ λαβὼν αὐτὸ ὁ δοῦλος τοῦ θεοῦ Νικόλαος
ἐβάπτισεν αὐτὸ εἰς τὸ ὄνομα τοῦ πατρὸς καὶ τοῦ υἱοῦ
20 καὶ τοῦ ἁγίου πνεύματος, καὶ ἀνάδοχος αὐτοῦ ἐγένετο.
καὶ ἀπῆλθον εὐχαριστοῦντες τῷ θεῷ, τῷ δώσαντι αὐτοῖς
μετὰ τριάκοντα ἐνιαυτοὺς δι᾽ εὐχῶν τοῦ δούλου τοῦ θεοῦ
τέκνον.

41. Πάλιν ἦλθον δύο ἀνδρόγυνα πρὸς τὸν δοῦλον τοῦ
θεοῦ Νικόλαον ἀπὸ τῆς ἐνορίας τοῦ Σαβάνδου ἐκ τοῦ
35Α χωρίου Δαμασεῖ. καὶ ἤνεγκαν ἐν τῷ μοναστηρίῳ γυναῖ-
κα παρθένον βαστάζοντες, οὖσαν ξηρὰν καὶ μὴ δυναμέ-
5 νην κινῆσαί τι τῶν μελῶν αὐτῆς τοῦ σώματος τὸ σύνο-
λον· καὶ τῇδε ἦν ὄνομα Κυριακή. καὶ ἔρριψαν αὐτὴν εἰς
τοὺς πόδας τοῦ δούλου τοῦ θεοῦ Νικολάου, λέγοντες
αὐτῷ· ῾Δεόμεθα τῆς σῆς ἁγιωσύνης, ἐλέησον τὴν ἀθλίαν
ταύτην, ὅτι δεινῶς βασανίζει αὐτὴν ὁ δαίμων καὶ ὀλόξη-
10 ρον αὐτὴν ἐποίησεν. ἰδοὺ γὰρ ἔχει ἑπτὰ ἔτη μὴ δυναμέ-
νη κινῆσαί τι τῶν μελῶν τοῦ σώματος αὐτῆς τὸ σύνολον.᾽ καὶ λέγει ὁ δοῦλος τοῦ θεοῦ Νικόλαος· ῞Εὰν πιστεύητε ἐξ ὅλης τῆς καρδίας ὑμῶν πρὸς τὸν κύριον ἡμῶν
᾽Ιησοῦν Χριστὸν καὶ εἰς τὴν δύναμιν τῆς ἁγίας Σιών, ἔχει
15 ὁ κύριος αὐτὴν θεραπεῦσαι ψυχῇ καὶ σώματι.᾽ καὶ λέγουσιν αὐτῷ· ῾Πιστεύομεν τῷ θεῷ καὶ τῇ σῇ ἁγιωσύνῃ ὅτι,
ἐὰν θέλῃς, δύνασαι αὐτὴν ἀναστῆσαι τάχιον. ἰδοὺ γὰρ
ἔχει ἑπτὰ ἔτη *ὀλόξηρος* κολαζομένη ὑπὸ τοῦ διαβόλου.᾽

compassion for us and grant us fruit." And the servant of God Nicholas said to them: "If you believe with all your heart in my Lord Jesus Christ, he will grant [it] to you." And they said to him: "We trust in God, that through your prayers God can grant [it] to us." And he stood and prayed for a long time, and taking oil from the lamp, he marked them with the sign of the cross, in the name of the Father and the Son and the Holy Spirit, and he sent them away. And a year later they returned with a male child. And the servant of God Nicholas took him, and baptized him in the name of the Father and of the Son and of the Holy Spirit, and became his godfather. And they went away thanking God, Who had given them a child after thirty years through the prayers of the servant of God.

41. Then again a married couple came to the servant of God Nicholas from the district of Sabandos, from the hamlet Damasei. And they carried with them and brought into the monastery an unmarried woman who was withered and unable to move the limbs of her body at all. And her name was Kyriake. And they cast her down at the feet of the servant of God Nicholas saying to him: "We beseech Your Holiness, have mercy on this wretch, since the Devil is tormenting her grievously and has made her wither away altogether. See, for seven years she has been unable to move the limbs of her body at all." And the servant of God Nicholas said: "If you believe with all your heart in our Lord Jesus Christ and in the power of Holy Sion, the Lord will cure her in soul and in body." And they said to him: "We trust in God and in Your Holiness that, if you so wish, you can raise her forthwith. For lo, for seven years she has been wholly withered and tormented by the Devil."

71

42. Ὁ δὲ δοῦλος τοῦ θεοῦ Νικόλαος, ἀκούσας ταῦτα παρὰ τῶν γονέων αὐτῆς, ἐσπλαγχνίσθη ἐπ᾽ αὐτήν, καὶ σταθεὶς προσηύξατο λέγων· ‘«Ὁ θεὸς ὁ αἰώνιος, ὁ τῶν κρυπτῶν γνώστης,» σὺ εἶ ὁ τυφλῶν ὀφθαλμοὺς φωτίζων
5 καὶ κωφῶν ὦτα ἀνοίγων καὶ γλώσσας ἀλάλων εἰς φωνὴν ἀνάγων καὶ λύων πάντα σύνδεσμον τοῦ πονηροῦ· ὁ τὰ παραλελυμένα μέλη διορθωσάμενος καὶ νῦν ὁ αὐτὸς εἶ, κύριε Ἰησοῦ Χριστέ, καὶ πλὴν σοῦ οὐκ ἔστιν ἄλλος. ἐλθέ, κύριε, καὶ ἐπὶ τὸ πλάσμα σου τοῦτο, καὶ φώτισον
10 τὴν σκοτισθεῖσαν ψυχὴν ὑπὸ τοῦ ἀλλοτρίου, καὶ δίωξον πᾶν φαῦλον καὶ πονηρὸν δαιμόνιον ἀπ᾽ αὐτῆς, καὶ ἄνοιξον τὸ στόμα αὐτῆς, διορθωσάμενος πᾶν μέλος τοῦ σώματος αὐτῆς· ἵνα δοξάσῃ σέ, τὸν μόνον ἀληθινὸν καὶ
36Α ζῶντα θεόν, καὶ κύριον ἡμῶν Ἰησοῦν Χριστόν, ᾧ ἡ δόξα
15 εἰς τοὺς αἰῶνας, ἀμήν.’ τελειώσαντος δὲ αὐτοῦ τὴν εὐχήν, θελήματι τοῦ θεοῦ ὑγιὴς ἐγένετο ἡ παρθένος ἀπὸ τῆς ὥρας ἐκείνης, καὶ ἀπῆλθεν εἰς τὸν οἶκον αὐτῆς δοξάζουσα τὸν θεόν.

43. Ἐν μιᾷ οὖν τῶν ἡμερῶν εἰσῆλθεν δαίμων εἰς τὸ κελλίον, ἐν ᾧ διῆγεν ὁ μακάριος Νικόλαος, καὶ ἔστη ἐν μέσῳ, μετασχηματισθεὶς εἰς ἄγγελον θεοῦ. ἰδὼν δὲ αὐτὸν ὁ δοῦλος τοῦ θεοῦ Νικόλαος λέγει αὐτῷ· ‘Τίς εἶ καὶ τί
5 εἰσῆλθες ὧδε;’ καὶ ἀποκριθεὶς ὁ δαίμων λέγει αὐτῷ· ‘Ἐγώ εἰμι ἄγγελος κυρίου, καὶ ἀπέστειλέν με ὁ κύριος, ἰδεῖν σε, τί ποιεῖς.’ ὁ δὲ μακάριος καὶ ὅσιος *τοῦ θεοῦ* Νικόλαος, νοήσας τὴν κακότεχνον γνώμην τοῦ μισοκάλου διαβόλου, κατασφραγισάμενος λέγει αὐτῷ· ‘Οἶδά
10 σε, τίς εἶ, ὦ ταλαίπωρε· ἔξελθε ἀπὸ τοῦ κελλίου τάχιον.’ ἀποκριθεὶς δὲ ὁ δαίμων λέγει αὐτῷ· ‘Τί γάρ σοι ποιῶ; ἔασόν με μικρὸν ὑπὸ τὴν στέγην σου, ἵνα ἀναπαύσω καὶ διδάξω σε τὸ θέλημά μου.’ ὁ δὲ δοῦλος τοῦ θεοῦ ἐπετίμησεν αὐτῷ λέγων· ‘Ἐν τῷ ὀνόματι τοῦ κυρίου μου Ἰησοῦ Χρι-

42. The servant of God Nicholas, when he heard these things from her parents, was moved with compassion for her, and stood and prayed saying: "O eternal God, 'Who knowest things hidden,' Thou art He Who lighteth the eyes of the blind and openeth the ears of the deaf, and leadeth the tongues of the dumb to sound, and looseneth all bonds of the Evil One. Even now, Thou art He Who hath restored the paralytic limbs, Lord Jesus Christ, and there is no other than Thou. Come, Lord, to this Thy creature, and lighten her soul which has been darkened by the Alien, and drive out every mean and evil devil from her, and open her mouth and restore every limb of her body, so that she may glorify Thee, the only true and living God and our Lord Jesus Christ, for Whom there is glory for ever and ever. Amen." When he had finished his prayer, by the will of God the young woman was cured from that very hour, and she departed to her home glorifying God.

43. Then one day, a demon entered the cell in which the blessed Nicholas lived, and stood in the middle, transformed into an angel of God. When the servant of God Nicholas saw him, he said to him: "Who are you, and why did you come in here?" And the demon answered, saying to him: "I am an angel of the Lord, and the Lord sent me to look and see what you are doing." The blessed Nicholas, God's holy man, recognizing the scheming intent of the demon, the hater of good, crossed himself and said to him: "I know who you are, O wretch. Be gone from the cell forthwith." And the demon answered, saying to him: "But what [harm] am I doing to you? Let me stay for a bit under your roof, so that I may rest and explain to you my design." But the servant of God rebuked him, saying: "In the name of my Lord Jesus Christ, go out right

15 στοῦ ἔξελθε ταχέως ἔξω, δαίμων ἐπικατάρατε.' καὶ κρά-
ξας ὁ δαίμων λέγει· 'Εἰ καὶ ἔνθεν με ἐκβάλλεις, οὐ μή
σου ἀναχωρήσω.' καὶ ἄφαντος ἐγένετο ἀπὸ τῆς ὥρας
ἐκείνης.

44. Καὶ πάλιν μετὰ μικρὸν εἰσῆλθεν ἐν τῷ μαγειρείῳ. καὶ
εὑρὼν τὸν ἀδελφὸν τοῦ ὁσίου ποιοῦντα ὑπηρεσίαν, λέγει
αὐτῷ· 'Σὺ τί θλίβῃ ὧδε καὶ μοχθεῖς, καὶ οὐκ ἀναπαύῃ
ἐν τῷ κελλαρίῳ ἔσω μετὰ τοῦ ἀδελφοῦ σου; ἐκεῖνος γὰρ
5 ἀνάπαυσιν ἔχει, καὶ σὺ θλίβῃ σεαυτόν. πρῶτος γὰρ ὢν
ἐκείνου εἰς τὰ ἔτη, οὐκ ἔχεις οὕτως βαστάξαι καὶ ὑπο-
μεῖναι τὰς θλίψεις ταύτας.' καὶ ἠγρίωσεν τὸν ἄκακον
καὶ δοῦλον τοῦ θεοῦ Ἀρτεμᾶν. καὶ μετὰ μικρὸν ἐγένετο
χρεία τῷ δούλῳ τοῦ θεοῦ Νικολάῳ, καὶ εἰσῆλθεν εἰς τὸ
37Α 10 μαγειρεῖον λαλῆσαι τῷ αὐτοῦ ἀδελφῷ, *ὅτι ἐάν τι ἔχῃ* ἔτοι-
μον εἰς τὸ ἄριστον τῶν ξένων. καὶ θυμωθεὶς ὁ *τούτου*
ἀδελφὸς ὑπὸ τοῦ διαβόλου λέγει αὐτῷ· 'Οὐκέτι ἀνέχομαί
σου οὕτως *ποιοῦντα*, ἵνα σὺ ἀνάπαυσιν ἔχῃς ἔσω, καὶ
ἐγὼ μοχθῶ καὶ θλίβομαι καθ' ἑκάστην ἡμέραν.' ὁ δὲ δοῦ-
15 λος τοῦ θεοῦ Νικόλαος, νοήσας τὴν κακότεχνον γνώμην
τοῦ διαβόλου, λέγει ἐν ἑαυτῷ ὅτι· "Ὁ ἐμοὶ παριστάμενος
ἐν τῷ κελλίῳ καὶ εἰπών μοι ὅτι· «Οὐ μὴ ἀναχωρήσω σοι,
ἀλλὰ πολλά σοι ἐνδείξομαι,» ἐκεῖνός ἐστιν ὁ ἀγριώσας
τὸν ἀδελφόν μου.' καὶ στὰς ηὔξατο. μετὰ δὲ *τὸ* πληρῶ-
20 σαι τὴν εὐχὴν ὁ δοῦλος τοῦ θεοῦ Νικόλαος, ἐπυρώθη ὁ
δαίμων, καὶ ἐξέρχεται ἀπὸ τοῦ μαγειρείου, κράζων καὶ
βλασφημῶν καὶ λέγων· "Ὦ ἀπὸ τοῦ Νικολάου, ὅτι πανταχόθεν με διώκει καὶ οὐκ ἐᾷ μέ τι ἐργάσασθαι τοῖς ἔρ-
γοις μου. ἐγὼ γὰρ ἐνόμιζον, ὅτι κἂν εἰς τὸν ἀδελφὸν
25 αὐτοῦ χωρῆσαι εἶχον, καὶ πανταχόθεν κατάγελως γέγονα.' ὁ δὲ δοῦλος τοῦ θεοῦ Νικόλαος, ἀκούσας ταῦτα
παρὰ τοῦ διαβόλου, ἐπετίμησεν αὐτῷ. καὶ ἄφαντος ἐγένετο ἀπὸ τῆς ὥρας ἐκείνης.

away, O accursed demon." And the demon cried out, saying: "Even though you throw me out of here, I will not leave you." And he vanished from sight from that very hour.

44. But, again, shortly afterwards he entered the kitchen. And he found the brother of the saint doing his service, and he said to him: "You, there, why are you wearing yourself out here with so much work, and not resting inside the cell along with your brother? For he is resting while you are wearing yourself out. For you are more advanced in years, and you should not have to endure so much or submit to this wear and tear." And he filled the innocent servant of God Artemas with rage. And a short while later the servant of God Nicholas had to attend to a piece of business, and he came into the kitchen to discuss with his brother whether the latter had anything ready for the visitors' morning meal. And his brother, riled up by the Devil, said to him: "I can no longer put up with these ways of yours, that you relax inside and I toil and wear myself out every single day." The servant of God Nicholas, recognizing the scheming intent of the Devil, said to himself: "That one who stood before me in the cell and said to me: 'I will never leave you, but will show you many things,' he is the same as the one who has filled my brother with rage." And he stood praying. When the servant of God Nicholas finished the prayer, the demon was inflamed, and left the kitchen crying out and cursing, saying: "O away from Nicholas, who drives me out from everywhere, and does not let me go about my business. For I thought that I at least would be able to enter into his brother, and [instead] I have become a laughing stock everywhere." The servant of God Nicholas, when he heard these things from the Devil, rebuked him. And the Devil vanished from sight from that very hour.

45. Πάλιν ἐν μιᾷ τῶν ἡμερῶν τεχνιτῶν πλειόνων ἐργαζο-
μένων ἐν τῷ εὐκτηρίῳ οἴκῳ, εἰσέρχεται ὁ δοῦλος τοῦ
θεοῦ Νικόλαος πρὸς τὸν αὐτοῦ ἀδελφὸν καὶ δευτεράριον, λέγων αὐτῷ· 'Πόσους ἄρτους ἔχεις, ἵνα παραθῶμεν
5 τῷ δείπνῳ τοῖς κάμνουσιν τεχνίταις;' λέγει αὐτῷ ὁ ἀδελφὸς αὐτοῦ· 'Εἷς ἄρτος ἔστιν μόνος, καὶ τί ἐστιν εἰς το-
σούτους;' ἦσαν γὰρ πάντες τὸν ἀριθμὸν ὀγδοήκοντα
τρεῖς. ὁ δὲ δοῦλος τοῦ θεοῦ Νικόλαος ἔστη ἐν τῇ προσευχῇ καὶ λέγει· 'Φέρε μοι τὸν ἄρτον, ὃν ἔχεις, ἐνθάδε.' καὶ
10 λαβὼν εὐλόγησεν, καὶ κλάσας παρέθηκεν τῷ ὄχλῳ. καὶ
πάντων κορεσθέντων, περιέσσευσεν ἐκ τοῦ ἑνὸς ἄρτου
κλάσματα, καὶ ἐπῆραν ἐκ τῶν ἐννέα τραπεζῶν κανίσκια
τρία. ἰδὼν δὲ ὁ αὐτοῦ ἀδελφὸς καὶ δευτεράριος τὴν δόξαν τοῦ θεοῦ, ὅτι διὰ τοῦ ἑνὸς ἄρτου πάντες ἐχορτάσθη-
15 σαν καὶ ἔτι περιέσσευσεν, ἔμφοβος γενάμενος οὐκέτι ἀν-
τειπεῖν ἠδυνήθη τῷ δούλῳ τοῦ θεοῦ.

38A **46.** Πάλιν δὲ μετὰ ἡμέρας ὀλίγας, εὐχομένου τοῦ δούλου
τοῦ θεοῦ Νικολάου ἐν τῇ ὥρᾳ τοῦ μεσονυκτίου, εἰσελθὼν
ἐν τῷ κελλαρίῳ ἡσύχασεν μικρὸν μετὰ Ἀρτεμᾶ τοῦ
αὐτοῦ ἀδελφοῦ καὶ δευτεραρίου. ἦλθεν ἀκάθαρτος δαί-
5 μων, νομίζων, φησίν, φαντάσαι τοὺς δούλους τοῦ θεοῦ.
ἐγένετο γὰρ ὡς ἄνθρωπος *φοβερός*, καὶ ἤρχετο ἀπὸ τοῦ
ἀνωγέου καταβῆναι τὴν κλίμακα. λέγει δὲ ὁ αὐτοῦ ἀδελφὸς καὶ δευτεράριος τῷ ἀββᾷ Νικολάῳ· 'Τίς ἐστιν ὁ κα-
τερχόμενος τὴν κλίμακα, πάτερ;' καὶ λέγει ὁ δοῦλος τοῦ
10 θεοῦ Νικόλαος· 'Θεωρεῖς αὐτὸν τίς ἐστιν;' ἀποκριθεὶς
δὲ λέγει· 'Οὐχί, κύριε, ἀλλὰ μόνον ψόφον αὐτοῦ ἀκούω.'
καὶ λέγει ὁ δοῦλος τοῦ θεοῦ· 'Μὴ φοβηθῇς, τέκνον. οὐ
γάρ ἐστιν ἄνθρωπος, ἀλλ' ὁ διάβολός ἐστιν, ὁ ἀπ' ἀρχῆς
ἔνεδρος τῶν δούλων τοῦ θεοῦ.'

45. Again, one day, when many craftsmen were working on the shrine, the servant of God Nicholas came up to his brother the *deuterarios* saying to him: "How many loaves of bread do you have that we can serve to the working craftsmen for supper?" His brother said to him: "There is only one loaf and what is that among so many?" For they numbered eighty-three in all. The servant of God Nicholas stood in prayer and said: "Bring me the loaf which you have in here." And he took and blessed it, broke it, and served it to the crowd. And when everyone had eaten enough, there remained fragments of the one loaf left over, and they collected three baskets from the nine tables. When his brother the *deuterarios* saw the glory of God, how everyone was filled out of the one loaf, with some still left over, he was awestruck and could no longer gainsay the servant of God.

46. Again, a few days later, when the servant of God Nicholas was praying at the hour of the midnight service, he came into the cell and rested a moment with his brother the *deuterarios* Artemas. There came an unclean demon, hoping, [as] he said [to himself], to delude the servants of God. For he took the form of a fearsome man and he started down the stairs from the floor above. His brother the *deuterarios* said to Father Nicholas: "Who is that coming down the stairs, father?" And the servant of God Nicholas said: "Can you make out who it is?" And he answered, saying: "Not at all, Lord, I only hear his footsteps." And the servant of God said: "Be not afraid, child. For this is not a man, but the Devil, he who from the beginning has been laying in wait for the servants of God."

47. Μιᾷ οὖν τῶν ἡμερῶν ἡσυχάζοντός μου ἐν τῷ κελλίῳ, εἶδον ὀπτασίαν, ἄγγελον κυρίου ἔφιππον καθεζόμενον καὶ λέγοντά μοι· «Δεῦρο, ὑπηρέτα τοῦ Χριστοῦ, ἴδε τὰ μέλλοντα γίνεσθαι εἰς τὸν κόσμον ὅλον· ὅτι καιρὸς τοῦ
5 θερισμοῦ πάρεστιν κατὰ κέλευσιν κυρίου τοῦ θεοῦ, καὶ ἀπέστειλέν με πρὸς σέ, δοῦναι σοι ὅπλα θερισμοῦ.» ἐγὼ δὲ ἔντρομος γενάμενος ἀκούσας τοῦ ἀγγέλου οὕτως, καὶ λέγω αὐτῷ· «Κύριε, τίς εἶ, ὅτι ἐμοὶ τῷ ἁμαρτωλῷ ἀπεστάλης, λαλῆσαι καὶ διακονῆσαί μοι περὶ θερισμοῦ;»
10 καὶ λέγει μοι· «Ἐγώ εἰμι ὁ ἄγγελος ὁ κρατῶν τὰ δρέπανα τοῦ θερισμοῦ. καὶ ἀπέστειλέν με κύριος ὁ θεός, δοῦναί σοι ἐκ τῶν δρεπάνων τούτων ἕνα, ὅτι ὁ καιρὸς τοῦ θερισμοῦ μέλλει ἔρχεσθαι ἐπὶ τὸν κόσμον ὅλον καὶ δεῖ σε ἔχειν ὅπλον καὶ σφραγίζειν τὸ θέρος καὶ παραδιδόναι.»
15 καὶ ἤγγισα τῷ ἀγγέλῳ, ἰδεῖν τὰ ὅπλα. καὶ βλέπω δῆθεν τρία δρέπανα, ἔχοντα τὸ πλάτος πέντε πήχεις καὶ τὸ μῆκος δέκα πέντε, καὶ ἐψηλάφησα τὰ τρία δρέπανα. καὶ λέγω τῷ ἐμῷ ἀδελφῷ· «Δεῦρο, ἀδελφέ, δῶμεν αὐτῷ
39Α τρεῖς εὐλογίας.» καὶ λέγει μοι· «Διὰ τί θέλεις, ἵνα δώσω-
20 μεν αὐτῷ τρεῖς εὐλογίας;» καὶ παρεγόγγυσεν.᾽ καὶ λέγει αὐτῷ ὁ δοῦλος τοῦ θεοῦ· ᾽Τρεῖς εὐλογίας οὐ θέλεις ἵνα αὐτῷ δῶμεν; ὄντως καὶ δύο περιστερὰς λαμβάνει καὶ οὕτως ὁδεύει.᾽ ᾽καὶ δῆθεν ἀνέστη ὡς γενναῖος στρατιώτης, καὶ ἐκάθισεν ἐν τῷ ἵππῳ αὐτοῦ, καὶ ἀπῆλθεν.᾽

48. Ἐγὼ δὲ ἔντρομος ἐγενόμην, καὶ ἀπὸ τοῦ φόβου διυπνίσθην. καὶ ἐγερθεὶς λέγω τῷ ἐμῷ ἀδελφῷ· «Δεῦρο, ἀδελφέ, σήμερον πλείους ψαλμοὺς εἴπωμεν εἰς τὸν ὄρθρον, ὅτι μέγαν φόβον εἶδον ἐν τῇ νυκτὶ ταύτῃ καὶ τρέμει μου
5 ἡ ψυχή.» καὶ λέγει μοι· «Τί εἶδες, πάτερ;» καὶ λέγω αὐτῷ ὅτι· «Εἶδον τὸν κόσμον μέλλοντα τελευτᾶν καὶ ὅτι

47. "So one day when I was resting in the cell, I had a vision of an angel of the Lord seated on horseback and saying to me: 'Come here, O minister of Christ, behold what shall come to pass to the whole world, for the time of harvest is at hand, by the command of the Lord God; and He sent me to you, to give you tools for the harvest.' I myself began to tremble when I heard the angel [speaking] thus, and I said to him: 'Lord, who art thou, that thou hast been sent down to me the sinner, to speak to me and to assist me regarding the harvest?' And he said to me: 'I am the angel who wields the sickles for the harvest. And the Lord God sent me to give you one of these sickles, since the time of harvest is at hand for the whole world, and you must have a tool and seal up the harvest and give it over.' And I drew near to the angel, to see the tools. And I saw, as it were, three sickles, five cubits in width, and fifteen cubits in length and I touched the three sickles. And I said to my brother: 'Come here, brother, let us give him three blessed loaves.' And he said to me: 'Why do you want us to give him three blessed loaves?' And he grumbled." And the servant of God said to him: "You do not want us to give him three loaves? Truly, he will take two doves as well, and so be on his way." "And the angel rose up, or so it seemed, noble soldier that he was, and he mounted his horse and rode away."

48. "I began to tremble and awoke out of fear. And having awakened, I said to my brother: 'Come here, brother, today let us sing more Psalms at Matins, for I saw something mighty terrifying last night, and my soul is trembling.' And he said to me: 'What did you see, Father?' And I said to him: 'I saw the world about to end, and that

79

διὰ τῆς χειρὸς ἡμῶν ἐκζητεῖ αὐτὰ ὁ κύριος ἐσφραγισμέ-
να.»' καὶ περὶ τούτου οὐκ ἐμέλησεν τῷ ἀδελφῷ αὐτοῦ,
ὅτι ἀλήθειαν λέγει. ὁ δὲ ἀββᾶς Νικόλαος μετὰ δακρύων
10 εἰσῆλθεν εἰς τὸν ὄρθρον, παρακαλῶν τὸν θεόν, ἵνα ἐπι-
δείξῃ αὐτῷ κύριος ὁ θεὸς τὰ περὶ τῆς ὀπτασίας αὐτοῦ,
τί ἐστιν.

49. ῾Καὶ μεθ᾽ ἡμέρας ὀλίγας εἶδον τὸ μέγα θυσιαστήριον
κολοβόν, ἐπινεύοντα τὸ δεξιὸν μέρος. καὶ ἐγγισάμην,
προσκυνῆσαι τῷ θυσιαστηρίῳ. καὶ ἀναβλέψας ἄνω εἰς
τὸν κούκουλλον, καὶ ἦν ἐξάερα. καὶ διαστρέφομαι εἰς
5 τὸν οἶκον τὸν βασιλικόν, καὶ ἦν στάζοντα εἰς ὅλον τὸν
οἶκον. καὶ δῆθεν ἐσυνάγετο τὸ ὕδωρ εἰς τὸν μέγαν πυλε-
ῶνα καὶ ἐξήρχετο ἔξω τοῦ πυλῶνος. καὶ ἀπὸ τοῦ φόβου καὶ τοῦ ἀγῶνος γέγονα ὡς ἐξ ὕπνου ἐξεγερθείς, καὶ
λέγω τῷ ὑπηρέτῃ μου· «Μεγάλα σημεῖα δεικνύει μοι ὁ
10 κύριος ἐν ὀπτασίαις, καὶ τί ἐστιν οὐκ οἶδα. δῶμεν οὖν
δόξαν τῷ θεῷ καὶ παρακαλέσωμεν τὸν κύριον ἡμῶν
Ἰησοῦν Χριστόν.»'

40Α **50.** Καὶ μεθ᾽ ἡμέρας ἑπτὰ κατέρχεται ἄγγελος κυρίου
καὶ φαίνεται τῷ δούλῳ τοῦ θεοῦ Νικολάῳ ἐν σχήματι
στρατιώτου, καὶ λέγει αὐτῷ· ῾Ἐπειδὴ ἐχαρίσατό σοι κύριος ὁ θεὸς δι᾽ ἀποκαλύψεως θεωρεῖν τὰ ἔργα τοῦ θεοῦ,
5 δεῦρο, φανερώσω σοι τὰς ὀπτασίας τῶν ἀγγέλων.' καὶ
εἶπεν αὐτῷ· ῾Σὺ γὰρ τίς εἶ;' καὶ λέγει αὐτῷ· ῾Ἐγώ εἰμι
Μιχαὴλ ὁ ἀρχάγγελος, ὁ διακονῶν σοι καθ᾽ ἑκάστην
ἡμέραν. καὶ ἐκέλευσέν μοι κύριος ὁ θεὸς φανερῶσαί σοι
τὰ μέλλοντα γενέσθαι εἰς τὸν κόσμον ὅλον. πέπεισμαι
10 δέ, ὅτι αὐτὸς πιστεύεις τῷ θεῷ· ἀλλὰ χρὴ τοὺς ἀδελφούς
σου πάντας ἐπιδιδάσκειν σε καὶ ἐπιλύειν αὐτοῖς διὰ τῶν
γραφῶν τὰ μέλλοντα. ἀπεστάλην φανερῶσαί σοι τὸν φό-

this be sealed up by my hand.'" And his brother did not give thought [to the fact] that he spoke the truth about this. But Father Nicholas went to Matins in tears, beseeching God that the Lord God would clarify to him the meaning of his vision.

49. "And a few days later, I saw the high altar truncated and tilting over toward the right. And I drew near, to worship the altar. And I looked up into the conch, and it was open to the sky. And I turned around to the main nave [?], and [water] was dripping in the whole nave [?]. And the water, so it seemed, collected at the great porch and flowed out from the porch. And I was aroused as though from sleep by the fear and agony, and I said to my attendant: 'The Lord shows me great signs in visions, and what they are, I know not. Therefore, let us give praise to God and beseech our Lord Jesus Christ.'"

50. And seven days later the angel of the Lord came down and appeared to the servant of God Nicholas in the garb of a soldier and said to him: "Since the Lord God has granted to you that you should contemplate the works of God through a revelation, come here, I will make visions of the angels manifest to you." And Nicholas said to him: "But who art thou?" And he said to him: "I am Michael the archangel, who ministers unto you every day. And the Lord God commanded me to reveal to you what shall come to pass to the whole world. Now, I am persuaded that you yourself have faith in God. But you must teach all your brethren as well, and expound to them the future through the Scriptures. I was sent to reveal to you the terror of God that is to come later. The one whom you saw coming on

βον τοῦ θεοῦ τὸν ὕστερον. ὃν εἶδες ἔφιππον ἐλθῶτα καὶ
ἔχοντα δρέπανα, ἄγγελος κυρίου ἐστίν· καὶ ἀπεστάλη
15 φανερῶσαί σοι τὰ μέλλοντα ἔρχεσθαι εἰς τὸν κόσμον,
καὶ πῶς μέλλουσιν παραδίδοσθαι αἱ ψυχαὶ τῶν ἀνθρώπων τοῖς ἁγίοις, καὶ οἱ ἅγιοι πῶς προσφέρουσιν αὐτὰς
τῷ θεῷ. καὶ ἐδόθη σοι εὔχεσθαι ὑπὲρ τῶν ψυχῶν τῶν μελ-
λόντων παραδίδοσθαι ἐκ τῆς Λυκίας.'

51. Ταῦτα ἀκούσας ὁ δοῦλος τοῦ θεοῦ Νικόλαος παρὰ
τοῦ ἀγγέλου λέγει αὐτῷ· "Ἐγὼ ἄνθρωπός εἰμι ἁμαρτωλός, καὶ πῶς δύναμαι ταῦτα ποιῆσαι;' καὶ ἀποκριθεὶς
ὁ ἄγγελος λέγει αὐτῷ· 'Τὰ δρέπανα, ἃ εἶδες, δύναμις
5 καὶ σφραγὶς κυρίου εἰσίν. καὶ ἐδόθη σοι, ἵνα διὰ τῶν
χειρῶν σου δίδονται αὐτοῖς αἱ ψυχαὶ τῶν ἀνθρώπων, ὅτι
ὡς θέρος παρέστη ἡ θνῆσις. τὸ γὰρ θέρος θνῆσίς ἐστιν
πρὸ τῆς συντελείας τῇ γενεᾷ τῶν ἀνθρώπων.' ταῦτα δὲ
10 εἰπὼν ὁ ἄγγελος τῷ δούλῳ τοῦ θεοῦ Νικολάῳ, ἀπῆλθεν
ἀπ' αὐτοῦ.

52. Καὶ εἴσω ἡμερῶν τεσσαράκοντα ἦλθεν ἡ θνῆσις τῶν
ἀνθρώπων. ἐποίησεν δὲ ἀρχὴν πρώτην ἐν τῇ μητροπόλει
τῶν Μυρέων, καὶ ἦν θλῖψις τῆς τῶν ἀνθρώπων πτώσεως
μεγάλη σφόδρα. οἱ δὲ παρακείμενοι τῇ ἐνορίᾳ γεωργοί,
5 ἰδόντες τὴν τοῦ θεοῦ ἐξουσίαν, ἐδειλίασαν τοῦ ἀπιέναι
εἰς τὴν πόλιν, λέγοντες ὅτι· "Ἐὰν δῶμεν τόπον *τῇ πόλει*,
οὐκ ἂν ἀποθάνωμεν νῦν τῷ πάθει τούτῳ.' ἦν γὰρ τὸ πά-
θος τοῦ βομβῶνος, καὶ αὐθίωρον ἤτοι μονήμερον ἀπε-
41Α δίδουν τὴν ψυχὴν οἱ ἄνθρωποι. καὶ ἀνεχώρουν τῆς πό-
10 λεως οἱ γεωργοί, καὶ οὐκ εἶχον πόθεν ζῆσαι αὐτοὶ οἱ περί-
λοιποι ἐν τῇ πόλει· οὔτε γὰρ σῖτος ἢ ἄλευρος ἢ οἶνος,
οὔτε ξύλον, οὔτε τι τῶν λοιπῶν *τῶν* πρὸς θεραπείαν ζωῆς
κατήρχετο ἀπὸ τῶν γεωργῶν ἐν τῇ πόλει. καὶ ἦν στένω-
σις καὶ θλῖψις τῶν ἀναλωμάτων σφόδρα μεγάλη.

horseback and carrying sickles, is an angel of the Lord. And he was sent to reveal to you what is about to come to the world, and how the souls of men will be given over to the holy men, and how the holy men will offer them to God. And it was given to you to pray for these souls that will be given over from Lycia.''

51. When the servant of God Nicholas heard these things from the angel, he said to him: "I am a sinful man, and how can I do these things?" And the angel answered him, saying: "The sickles which you saw are the power and the seal of the Lord. And it was granted to you that through your hands the souls of men would be given to these [sickles], since the plague has arrived like unto a harvest. For the harvest is the plague coming to the race of men before the end of the world.'' Having said this to the servant of God Nicholas, the angel departed from him.

52. And the plague came to people within forty days. It had its first beginning in the metropolis of Myra, and there was exceeding great affliction over the deaths of men. When the neighboring farmers living in the district saw the power of God, they feared to go into the city, saying: "If we give the city wide berth, we will not die of this disease.'' For the disease was bubonic and people were expiring right away, that is, within a single day. And the farmers were withdrawing from the city, and the survivors in the city had no means of livelihood. For the farmers brought down into the city neither grain, nor flour, nor wine, nor wood, nor anything else needed for sustenance. And there was hardship and exceeding great affliction over the provisions.

53. Εἰσῆλθεν δὲ φήμη ἐν Μύροις τῇ μητροπόλει, καὶ ἔλε-
γον ὅτι· ''Ο ἀββᾶς τῆς ἁγίας Σιὼν οὐκ ἐᾷ τινα τῶν γεωργῶν κατέρχεσθαι ἐν τῇ πόλει.' ἀκούσας δὲ ταῦτα ὁ τότε
ὁσιώτατος ἀρχιεπίσκοπος Φίλιππος, ἐδήλωσεν τῷ τότε
5 ἄρχοντι τῆς ἐπαρχίας καὶ τοῖς πρωτεύουσιν, ὅτι ὁ δοῦλος τοῦ θεοῦ Νικόλαος ταῦτα ἐποίησεν. ὀργισθέντες δὲ
ἀπέστειλαν δύο κληρικοὺς εἰς τὸ μοναστήριον τῆς ἁγίας
Σιὼν πρὸς τὸν δοῦλον τοῦ θεοῦ Νικόλαον, παραγγείλαν-
τες μετὰ σπουδῆς δεδεμένον ἀγαγεῖν τὸν δοῦλον
10 τοῦ θεοῦ. οἱ δὲ ὑπηρέται τοῦ ἀρχιεπισκόπου, καταντή-
σαντες ἐν τῷ μοναστηρίῳ, λέγουσι τῷ δούλῳ τοῦ θεοῦ
Νικολάῳ· 'Συκοφαντίαι μεγάλαι ἐγένοντο κατὰ τοῦ
ἀγγέλου ὑμῶν [ἔμπροσθέν σου] πρὸς τὸν ἀρχιεπίσκο-
πον καὶ τὸν ἄρχοντα τῆς πόλεως· καὶ ἀπέστειλαν ἡμᾶς,
15 ὥστε κατενέγκαι σε δεδεμένον εἰς τὴν πόλιν.' καὶ λέγει
ὁ δοῦλος τοῦ θεοῦ· 'Οἶδα καὶ πέπεισμαι, ὅτι ταῦτα πάντα
ὁ διάβολος διέσπειρεν τοῖς ἀνθρώποις· ἀλλὰ πιστεύω
τῷ θεῷ ὅτι πατεῖται ὑφ' ἡμῶν τῶν ἐλαχίστων.' γνωστὸν
οὖν ἐγένετο ἐν τῇ Τραγλασσέων κώμῃ, ὅτι ὁ δοῦλος τοῦ
20 θεοῦ ἐσυκοφαντήθη ἐν τῇ πόλει καὶ ὅτι ἀνῆλθόν τινες
τῆς πόλεως κληρικοὶ ἀπὸ τοῦ ἀρχιεπισκόπου Φιλίππου
42A καὶ τοῦ ἄρχοντος, ὥστε δεδεμένον αὐτὸν καταγαγεῖν
ἀπὸ τοῦ μοναστηρίου. συνήχθησαν οὖν πάντες, λέγοντες
τῷ δούλῳ τοῦ θεοῦ Νικολάῳ ὅτι· 'Μὴ δόξῃ σοι κατελθεῖν
25 εἰς τὴν πόλιν, ὅτι μεγάλη ὀργὴ ἐπίκειται διὰ σὲ εἰς τὴν
πόλιν.'

54. Ὅτε οὖν ηὐδόκησεν ὁ θεὸς δοξάσαι τὸν δοῦλον
αὐτοῦ Νικόλαον, ἐπορεύθη εἰς τὸ εὐκτήριον τοῦ †ἀρχαγ-
γέλου εὐφήμου† ἐν Τραγαλασσῷ, καὶ ἔθυσεν ζυγὴν βοϊδίων, καὶ συγκαλεῖται πάντα τὸν λαόν. καὶ ἐγένετο εὐω-
5 χία καὶ χαρὰ μεγάλη. καὶ εὐφρανθέντες ἔδωκαν δόξαν
τῷ θεῷ τῷ δοξάζοντι τοὺς δοξάζοντας αὐτόν. καὶ ἀπ'

53. A rumor spread in the metropolis of Myra, and they said: "The Abbot of Holy Sion does not let any of the farmers go down to the city." When he heard these things, Philip, the most blessed archbishop of that time reported to the then governor of the province, and to the chief magistrates [of the city], that the servant of God Nicholas had done this. They grew angry and sent two clerics to the Monastery of Holy Sion to the servant of God Nicholas, with the command to make haste and have the servant of God brought in chains. The attendants of the archbishop arrived at the monastery and said to the servant of God Nicholas: "There have been serious denunciations [made] against Your Angelic Self before the archbishop and the governor of the city . And they sent us to have you brought down to the city in chains." And the servant of God said: "I know and am convinced that it was the Devil who sowed all these [slanders] among the people. But I have faith in God that the Devil will be trampled upon by us, the most lowly ones." So it became known in the village of the Traglassians, that the servant of God had been slandered in the city and that some city clerics had come up from Archbishop Philip and the governor, in order to have him brought down from the Monastery in chains. So they all gathered together, saying to the servant of God Nicholas: "Would you please not go down to the city, for there is much wrath in the city on your account."

54. When, therefore, it pleased God to honor his servant Nicholas, he journeyed to the shrine of the renowned Archangel [?] in Traglassos, and slaughtered a pair of oxen, and called together all the people. And there was feasting, and a great joy. And they made merry, and gave thanks to God, Who honors them that honor Him. And

ἐκεῖθεν ἐπορεύθη ἐν τῷ μοναστηρίῳ τοῦ ἁγίου Ἰωάννου
καὶ τῶν ὁσίων πατέρων Σαββατίου καὶ Νικολάου καὶ
Λέοντος, τῶν γεναμένων ἀρχιμανδριτῶν ἐν τῷ
10 Ἀκαλισσῷ. καὶ ἔθυσεν βοΐδια πέντε καὶ συγκαλεῖ πάντα
τὸν λαόν, καὶ ἔφαγον καὶ ἐνεπλήσθησαν, καὶ ἐδοξάσθη
ὁ θεὸς διὰ τοῦ δούλου αὐτοῦ Νικολάου. ἔτι δὲ τῇ ⟨ τοῦ
θεοῦ ⟩ χάριτι καὶ τῇ τοῦ ἁγίου πνεύματος παρρησίᾳ
φερόμενος εἰς πάσας τὰς παρακειμένας ἁγίας ἐκκλη-
15 σίας θυσίας ἐπέδωκεν εὐχαριστῶν τῷ θεῷ βοΐδια δέκα
ἕξ, πληρώσας τὴν προφητικὴν φωνὴν τοῦ ἁγίου Δαβίδ,
τὴν λέγουσαν· «ἀποδώσω σοι τὰς εὐχάς μου, ἃς διέστει-
λεν τὰ χείλη μου καὶ ἐλάλησεν τὸ στόμα μου ἐν τῇ θλίψει
μου.»

55. Καὶ ἐν ταῖς ἡμέραις ἐκείναις ἐπορεύθη ὁ δοῦλος τοῦ
θεοῦ Νικόλαος εἰς τὸ εὐκτήριον τοῦ ἁγίου Γεωργίου ἐν
43Α τῷ Πληνίῳ. καὶ ἦλθον μετὰ λιτανείας καὶ τῶν τιμίων
σταυρῶν καὶ ἀπήντησαν τῷ δούλῳ τοῦ θεοῦ οἱ ἀπὸ τοῦ
5 Πληνίου κληρικοὶ ἅμα τῷ φιλοχρίστῳ αὐτῶν λαῷ εἰς
τὸν †ἅγιον εὔφημον†. καὶ ἀπ᾽ ἐκεῖθεν ἠκολούθησεν
αὐτοῖς μετὰ ἑπτὰ βοϊδίων. καὶ ἀπελθόντες ἐν τῷ εὐκτηρίῳ τοῦ ἁγίου Γεωργίου ἔθυσεν ὁ δοῦλος τοῦ θεοῦ τοὺς
ἑπτὰ βόας. καὶ συνήχθησαν ὄχλοι, ὥστε γενέσθαι
10 στιβάδια διακόσια. ἐβάστασεν δὲ ὁ δοῦλος τοῦ θεοῦ
ὑπὲρ ἀναλωμάτων οἴνου μέτρα ἑκατὸν καὶ ἄρτους μοδίων τεσσαράκοντα. καὶ ἔφαγον πάντες καὶ ἐνεπλήσθησαν, καὶ ἐδόξασαν τὸν θεὸν τὸν δόντα χάριν τῷ δούλῳ
αὐτοῦ Νικολάῳ. καὶ περίσσευσεν οἴνου μέτρα ἑξήκοντα
15 καὶ ἄρτοι ἑκατὸν καὶ ἐλαίου μέτρα τέσσαρα. καὶ μετὰ
τὸ ἐμπλησθῆναι πάντες ἐδόξασαν τὸν θεὸν διὰ τοῦ
δούλου αὐτοῦ.

56. Μετὰ δὲ χρόνους δύο πνεῦμα ἅγιον φαίνεται τῷ
δούλῳ τοῦ θεοῦ Νικολάῳ ἐπὶ τὸ παραγενέσθαι εἰς τοὺς
παρακειμένους εὐκτηρίους ἁγίους οἴκους καὶ ποιῆσαι

from there he journeyed to the Monastery of Saint John, and of the holy fathers Sabbatios and Nicholas and Leo, the late archimandrites in Akalissos. And he slaughtered five oxen and called together all the people, and they ate and were filled, and God was glorified through His servant Nicholas. Furthermore, by the grace of [God] and by the boldness that the Holy Spirit [granted to him] he went to all the holy churches nearby, and gave thanks to God and offered up sixteen oxen, fulfilling the prophecy of holy David, which ran: "I will pay thee my vows, which my lips have uttered, and my mouth hath spoken in my trouble."

55. And in those days the servant of God Nicholas journeyed to the shrine of Saint George in Plenion. And the clerics from Plenion came along with their Christ-loving flock, singing litanies and carrying venerable crosses, and met the servant of God at the renowned Saint's [?] [shrine]. And he went along with them from there, along with seven oxen. And they went to the shrine of Saint George, where the servant of God slaughtered the seven oxen. And crowds gathered, so that there were two hundred place settings. The servant of God carried with him one hundred measures of wine and forty modii of bread as provisions. And they all ate and were filled, and they glorified God, Who gave grace to His servant Nicholas. And there were sixty measures of wine left over, as well as one hundred loaves of bread and four measures of olive oil. And after they were filled, they all glorified God through His servant.

56. Two years later, the Holy Spirit appeared to the servant of God Nicholas, [telling him] to visit the holy shrines nearby, and at each sanctuary to make a sacrificial offer-

87

καθ' ἕκαστον ἁγίασμα θυσίας ἀπὸ ζυγῆς βοϊδίων καὶ
5 δοξάσαι τὸν θεόν. τῇ οὖν ἡμέρᾳ ἐκείνῃ, ἐν ᾗ τὸ πνεῦμα
τὸ ἅγιον ἐφάνη αὐτῷ περὶ τῶν θυσιῶν, λέγει τῷ ἀδελφῷ
καὶ δευτεραρίῳ αὐτοῦ Ἀρτεμᾷ καὶ τοῖς ἀδελφοῖς πᾶσιν
ὅτι· 'Σήμερον βουλήσει τοῦ θεοῦ ἐξελθεῖν θέλω ἕως τοῦ
εὐκτηρίου τοῦ ἁγίου Γαβριὴλ εἰς Καρκάβω, ποιῆσαι τὸ
10 θέλημα τοῦ θεοῦ.' ἐβάστασεν δὲ ἀπὸ τοῦ μοναστηρίου
44Α νομίσματα * * * καὶ οἴνου μέτρα ἑβδομήκοντα καὶ σίτου
μόδια τριάκοντα. καὶ ἀπελθὼν εἰς τὸν προλεχθέντα ἔνδοξον οἶκον τοῦ ἁγίου Γαβριὴλ τοῦ ἀρχαγγέλου, καὶ ἔθυσεν τρία βοΐδια καὶ ἐκάλεσεν τὸν ἐκεῖ ὄντα λαὸν πάν-
15 τα. καὶ ἔφαγον καὶ ἐνεπλήσθησαν σφόδρα καὶ ἐδόξασαν τὸν θεὸν πάντες καὶ τὸν δοῦλον αὐτοῦ Νικόλαον.
καὶ περιέσσευσεν ἐξ αὐτῶν εὐλογία πολλή, ὥστε ἀπὸ
Καρκάβω ἀγαλλιώμενον τὸν δοῦλον τοῦ θεοῦ Νικόλαον
ἀπελθεῖν ἐν τῷ εὐκτηρίῳ οἴκῳ τοῦ ἁγίου Θεοδώρου εἰς
20 Καύσας. κἀκεῖ ἔθυσεν ζυγὴν βοϊδίων, καὶ συγκαλεσάμε-
νος πάντα τὸν ἐκεῖσε λαόν. καὶ ἐμπλησθέντες ἐδόξασαν κύριον τὸν θεόν. καὶ ἐκ τῆς περισσείας τοῦ ἁγίου
Θεοδώρου τῶν εὐλογιῶν ἀπ' ἐκεῖθεν παρεγένετο εἰς τὸν
εὐκτήριον οἶκον τοῦ ἁγίου ἀρχαγγέλου εἰς Νέαν Κώμην.
25 κἀκεῖ ἔθυσεν βοϊδίων ζυγὴν μίαν, καὶ συνεκάλεσεν πάντα τὸν ἐκεῖσε λαὸν ἀπὸ μικροῦ ἕως μεγάλου. καὶ ἐμπλησθέντες ἅπαντες ἐδόξασαν τὸν θεόν, καὶ ἐπερίσσευεν
ἡ τοῦ θεοῦ δωρεά.

57. Καὶ ἰδὼν ὁ δοῦλος τοῦ θεοῦ Νικόλαος τὴν περισσείαν
οὐκ ὀλίγην οὖσαν, ἐννοήσας ὅτι τὸ ἅγιον πνεῦμα τὸ
ὀφθὲν αὐτῷ μετ' αὐτοῦ ἐστιν, ἀπὸ Νέας Κώμης ἀπῆλθεν
εἰς τὸ εὐκτήριον τοῦ ἁγίου Ἀπφιανοῦ ἐν Παρταησσῷ·
5 κἀκεῖ ἔθυσεν βοϊδίων ζυγὴν μίαν, καὶ συγκαλεῖται πάντα
τὸν λαόν· καὶ ἔφαγον καὶ ἐνεπλήσθησαν καὶ ἐδόξασαν

ing of a pair of oxen and to glorify God. So on the very day on which the Holy Spirit appeared to him about the offerings, he said to his brother, the *deuterarios* Artemas, and to all the brethren: "Today by God's will I shall go as far as the shrine of Saint Gabriel in Karkabo, to do the will of God." He took from the monastery. . . .nomismata, seventy measures of wine, and thirty modii of grain. And he went off to the aforementioned glorious shrine of the holy Archangel Gabriel, and slaughtered three oxen, and summoned all the people of the place. And they ate and were well-filled, and they all glorified God and His servant Nicholas. And plenty of blessed bread was left over, so that Nicholas, the servant of God, left Karkabo rejoicing, and went to the shrine of Saint Theodore at Kausai. And there he slaughtered a pair of oxen, and called together all the people who were there. And when they were filled, they glorified the Lord God. And because so much of the loaves was left over at Saint Theodore, he went from there to the shrine of the holy Archangel in Nea Kome. And there he slaughtered one pair of oxen and called together all the people who were there, both young and old. And they were all filled, and glorified God, and God's gifts were in overabundance.

57. And when the servant of God Nicholas saw that what had been left over was considerable, he understood that the Holy Spirit, who had appeared to him, was with him; and he went from Nea Kome to the shrine of Saint Apphianos in Partaessos. And there he slaughtered one pair of oxen and called together all the people. And they ate,

τὸν θεόν. καὶ περιέσσευσεν εὐλογία μεγάλη, ὥστε τὸν
δοῦλον τοῦ θεοῦ ἐπὶ πλεῖον δοξάζειν τὸν θεόν. καὶ ἀπ᾽
ἐκεῖθεν κατῆλθεν εἰς τὸ εὐκτήριον τοῦ ἀρχαγγέλου καὶ
10 τοῦ ἁγίου Δημητρίου ἐν τῷ Συμβόλῳ. καὶ ἔθυσεν βοΐδια
45A δύο καὶ συγκαλεῖται πάντα τὸν λαόν, καὶ εὐφρανθέντες
ἐδόξασαν τὸν θεὸν διὰ τὴν πίστιν τοῦ δούλου τοῦ θεοῦ
Νικολάου. καὶ πληθυνθέντων τῶν ἀναλωμάτων, εὐχαριστῶν τῷ ἁγίῳ πνεύματι ἀπ᾽ ἐκεῖθεν ἐπορεύθη εἰς τὸ
15 εὐκτήριον τῆς Θεοτόκου εἰς τὸ Ναυτήν. καὶ ἔθυσεν κἀκεῖ
ζυγὴν βοϊδίων, καὶ συνεκάλεσεν πάντα τὸν ἐκεῖσε ὄντα λαόν, καὶ εὐφρανθέντες ἔδωκαν αἶνον τῷ θεῷ. καὶ
ἀπ᾽ ἐκεῖθεν ἐπορεύθη εἰς τὸ εὐκτήριον τῆς ἁγίας Εἰρήνης
εἰς Σερινῆ. κἀκεῖ ἔθυσεν ζυγὴν βοϊδίων, καὶ συγκαλεῖται
20 τὸν λαόν, καὶ εὐφρανθέντες ἔδωκαν αἶνον τῷ θεῷ. καὶ
ἀπ᾽ ἐκεῖθεν ἐπορεύθη εἰς τὸν εὐκτήριον οἶκον τοῦ ἀρχαγγέλου εἰς Τρεβένδας. κἀκεῖ ἔθυσεν βοϊδίων ζυγὴν μίαν,
καὶ ἐποίησεν δοχὴν μεγάλην, δοξάζων τὸν θεόν. καὶ ἀπ᾽
25 ἐκεῖθεν ἐπορεύθη εἰς τὸ Κάστελλον εἰς τὸν εὐκτήριον
οἶκον τοῦ ἁγίου Νικολάου. κἀκεῖ ἔθυσεν βοΐδια δύο, καὶ
εὐφράνθη πᾶς ὁ φιλόχριστος λαός, καὶ ἐδόξασαν τὸν
θεὸν διὰ τοῦ ὁσίου ἀνδρός. καὶ ἀπ᾽ ἐκεῖθεν ἐπορεύθη εἰς
τὸν εὐκτήριον οἶκον τῆς Μελίσσης ἐν Ἡμαλίσσοις.
30 κἀκεῖ ἔθυσεν βοΐδια δύο, καὶ συγκαλεῖται πάντα τὸν
λαόν, καὶ εὐφρανθέντες ἔδωκαν δόξαν τῷ θεῷ καὶ τῷ
δούλῳ αὐτοῦ Νικολάῳ. καὶ τότε, πληρώσας τὴν ἐπαγγε-
λίαν τοῦ ἁγίου πνεύματος, ἀγαλλιώμενος ἅμα τοῖς συν-
οῦσιν αὐτῷ ἀδελφοῖς διὰ εἴκοσι πέντε ἡμερῶν ἦλθεν εἰς
35 τὸ μοναστήριον αὐτοῦ εἰς τὴν ἁγίαν Σιών.

58. Καὶ ἐν ταῖς ἡμέραις ἐκείναις ἦν παλαιωθέντα τὸ
ἁγίασμα τοῦ ἁγίου Δανιὴλ ἐν τῷ Σαβάνδῳ καὶ συμπίπ-
τοντα. καὶ ἀπερχομένου τοῦ μακαρίου καὶ ὁσίου ἀνδρὸς

and were filled, and praised God. And there was much blessed bread left over, so that the servant of God praised God even more. And from there he came down to the shrine of the Archangel and of Saint Demetrios in Symbolon. And he slaughtered two oxen and called together all the people and, making merry, they glorified God through the faith of the servant of God Nicholas. And as provisions grew in abundance, he gave thanks to the Holy Spirit and journeyed from there to the shrine of the Virgin in Nauten. And there, too, he slaughtered a pair of oxen, and called together all the people of the place, and they made merry, and gave praise to God. And from there he journeyed to the shrine of Saint Irene [?] in Serine. And there he slaughtered a pair of oxen and called together all the local people, and they made merry and gave praise to God. And from there he journeyed to the shrine of the Archangel at Trebendai. And there he slaughtered one pair of oxen and gave a great feast, glorifying God. And from there he journeyed to Kastellon, to the shrine of Saint Nicholas. And there he slaughtered two oxen, and all the Christ-loving people made merry, and glorified God through the holy man. And from there he journeyed to the shrine of Melissa in Hemalissoi. And there he slaughtered two oxen, and called together all the people, and they made merry and gave glory to God and to His servant Nicholas. And then, having fulfilled the command [?] of the Holy Spirit, and rejoicing together with the brethren who had been with him, he arrived at his monastery at Holy Sion after twenty-five days.

58. And in those days, the sanctuary of Saint Daniel in Sabandos was about to collapse on account of old age. And on his way from his monastery to the splendid metropolis

91

Νικολάου ἀπὸ τοῦ μοναστηρίου κατὰ τὴν λαμπρὰν Μυ-
5 ρέων μητρόπολιν, ἔκαμψεν ἐν τῷ Καστέλλῳ ἐπὶ τὸ εὔξασθαι. καὶ εἰσελθὼν ἐν τῷ εὐκτηρίῳ τοῦ ἁγίου Δανιὴλ τοῦ
προφήτου καὶ ἰδών, ὅτι πτῶσιν ὑπομένει ὁ ἅγιος τοῦ θεοῦ
οἶκος, μετεκαλέσατο ἕνα τῶν κληρικῶν, ὀνόματι Νικόλαον, ἀπὸ τοῦ χωρίου Δαμασεῖ, ἅμα τῷ τότε τεχνίτῃ τῆς
10 οἰκοδομῆς, ὀνόματι Θεοτίμῳ. συνταξάμενος καὶ δώσας
αὐτοῖς εὐλογίαν, αὐτῇ τῇ ὥρᾳ ἔδωκεν Νικολάῳ τῷ δια-
κόνῳ ὑπὲρ τελειώσεως τοῦ ἔργου νομίσματα ὀγδοήκοντα ἥμισυ, προστάξας τὰ ἀναλώματα ρογεύεσθαι ἀπὸ
τοῦ εὐαγοῦς αὐτοῦ μοναστηρίου. καὶ ἐτελειώθη ὁ ἅγιος
15 οἶκος, καὶ πάντες εὐχαρίστησαν τῷ θεῷ διὰ τοῦ δούλου
αὐτοῦ Νικολάου.

46Α **59.** Καὶ μετὰ ταῦτα ἦλθεν εἰς προσευχὴν εἰς τὸ μοναστήριον τῆς ἁγίας Σιὼν πρὸς τὸν δοῦλον τοῦ θεοῦ Νικόλαον
ἀνδρόγυνον ἐκ τῆς Ἀρνεατῶν ἐνορίας, ᾧ ὄνομα Ἰωάννης μετὰ τῆς γαμετῆς αὐτοῦ, προσπίπτοντες τῷ δούλῳ
5 τοῦ θεοῦ καὶ λέγοντες ὅτι· 'Ἔχομεν σήμερον οἰκοῦντες
ἐν τῷ χωρίῳ ἡμῶν εἴκοσιν ἔτη. καὶ ἔστιν ὁ σπόρος τοῦ
χωρίου μοδίων εἴκοσι πέντε τοῦ μεγάλου καὶ οὐδέν ποτε
ἐποιήσαμεν περισσὸν τῶν εἴκοσι πέντε μοδίων. καὶ ἤλθαμεν προσκυνῆσαι τὸν θεὸν καὶ τὴν ἁγίαν Σιὼν καὶ τὴν
10 σὴν ἁγιωσύνην, ἵνα ὑπὲρ ἡμῶν τῶν ταπεινῶν παρακαλέ-
σῃς τὸν θεόν, ἵνα διὰ τῶν ὁσίων σου εὐχῶν ἐλεηθῶμεν.
ὅτι ἐπτωχεύσαμεν καὶ τῶν προσοδιῶν ἐξεπέσαμεν καὶ
‹ ὑπὸ › τῆς λιμοῦ φθειρόμεθα, οἰκοῦντες τὸ χωρίον ἐκεῖνο, καὶ κάμνοντες ἀποθνῄσκομεν, καὶ πῶς ζῆσαι οὐκ
15 ἔχομεν.' καὶ λέγει ὁ δοῦλος τοῦ θεοῦ Νικόλαος· 'Καὶ ἐγὼ
ἁμαρτωλός εἰμι ἄνθρωπος, ἐὰν δὲ ἔχητε πίστιν θεοῦ, ὁ
κύριος ὑμῖν δοῦναι ἔχει ὑπὲρ τῶν ἐτῶν ὧν ἐκοπώθητε.'
καὶ προσκυνήσαντες λέγουσιν αὐτῷ· 'Δοῦλε τοῦ θεοῦ,
ἡμεῖς πιστεύομεν τῷ θεῷ καὶ τῷ ἀγγέλῳ σου.' καὶ στα-
20 θεὶς ὁ δοῦλος τοῦ θεοῦ ηὔξατο ἐπὶ ὥρας δύο, καὶ λέγει
αὐτοῖς· 'Ὑπάγετε, καί, ὃ θέλει κύριος, ἔχει γενέσθαι.'

of Myra, the blessed and holy man Nicholas turned off to Kastellon in order to pray. And as he entered the shrine of Saint Daniel the Prophet, and saw that the holy house of God was about to collapse, he summoned one of the clerics, by the name of Nicholas, from the hamlet of Damasei, together with a man by the name of Theotimos, who at that time was the master builder. Taking leave of them, and giving them his blessing, he gave to the deacon Nicholas at that very time eighty and a half nomismata for the completion of the work [of restoration]. And he gave orders that the provisions be supplied from his venerable monastery. And the holy shrine was completed, and they all gave thanks to God through his servant Nicholas.

59. And after this, a married man from the district of Arneai came to the servant of God Nicholas to pray at the Monastery of Holy Sion: [a man] whose name was John, with his spouse. And they fell down before the servant of God, saying: "As of today, we have lived on our piece of land for twenty years. And this land requires twenty-five large modii of seed grain and never yet have we gotten more than twenty-five modii in return. And we have come to worship God, and Holy Sion and Your Holiness, so that you may beseech God for us, the humble ones, that we may find mercy through your blessed prayers. For we have been brought very low, have lost our income, and are wasting away with hunger, living on that piece of land; we are working ourselves to death, and are no longer able to eke out our livelihood." And the servant of God Nicholas said, "I, too, am a sinful man. But if you have faith in God, the Lord will recompense you for [all] those years of toil." And they made reverence, saying to him, "O servant of God, we believe in God and in your Angelic Self." And the servant of God stood praying for two hours, then said to them: "Go now, and what God wishes will come to pass."

60. Καὶ εἰς τὸ ἐπερχόμενον ἔτος ἔσπειραν τὸ αὐτὸ χωρίον, καὶ ἔβαλον τὸν αὐτὸν μοδισμόν. καὶ τελειωθέντος
τοῦ σπόρου καὶ θερισθείσης τῆς χώρας, συνήγαγεν ὁ
γεωργὸς τοὺς καρποὺς ἐκ τῆς αὐτῆς χώρας, μοδίους
5 ἑκατὸν εἴκοσι πέντε μεγάλους. καὶ εὐχαρίστησαν τῷ θεῷ
καὶ τῇ προσευχῇ τοῦ ὁσίου ἀνδρὸς Νικολάου, ὅτι δι᾽
αὐτῆς τοσαύτην εὐλογίαν ἔλαβον. ἐπιγνοὺς δὲ ὁ γεωργὸς
Ἰωάννης, ὅτι τοσαύτης εὐλογίας ἠξιώθη διὰ τῆς προσευχῆς τοῦ δούλου τοῦ θεοῦ Νικολάου, λέγει τῇ ἰδίᾳ γυ-
47A 10 ναικί· ᾽Δεῦρο, ἀπέλθωμεν καὶ προσπέσωμεν τῷ δούλῳ
τοῦ θεοῦ Νικολάῳ, ὅτι διὰ τῆς ὁσίας αὐτοῦ προσευχῆς
μεγάλης εὐλογίας ἠξίωσεν ἡμᾶς ὁ θεός.᾽ ἦλθον οὖν πρὸς
τὸν τοῦ θεοῦ δοῦλον Νικόλαον, καὶ ἔρριψαν ἑαυτοὺς εἰς
τοὺς πόδας αὐτοῦ, καὶ εὐχαριστοῦντες λέγουσιν ἅπαντα
15 τὰ γινόμενα σημεῖα διὰ τῶν ὁσίων αὐτοῦ εὐχῶν, καὶ πῶς
ἐπλήθυνεν ὁ θεὸς τοὺς καρποὺς τῆς χώρας αὐτῶν. καὶ
λέγει ὁ δοῦλος τοῦ θεοῦ· ῾Υπάγετε, εὐχαριστεῖτε τῷ θεῷ·
ὅτι ὅτε θελήσει ὁ θεός, δύναται τὰ ὀλίγα πληθῦναι καὶ
τὰ πολλὰ ἐλαττῶσαι.᾽ καὶ ἀπέλυσεν αὐτοὺς δοξάζον-
20 τας τὸν θεόν.

61. Καί τις ἀνὴρ ὀνόματι Κοσμᾶς, ὃς ἦν ἀναγνώστης
τῆς ἐνορίας Ἠνεανδῶν, ἀπὸ χωρίου Οὐάλω, ἦλθεν ἐν
τῷ μοναστηρίῳ τῆς ἁγίας Σιών, ἔχων πνεῦμα ἀκάθαρτον. καὶ ἦν ὁδηγούμενος ὑπὸ ἀνθρώπων δύο διὰ τὸ πα-
5 ραφρονεῖν αὐτόν. καὶ προσπεσόντες τῷ δούλῳ τοῦ θεοῦ
Νικολάῳ εἶπον· ᾽Δεόμεθά σου, τίμιε πάτερ, ἐλέησον τὸ
πλάσμα τοῦ θεοῦ, καὶ εὖξαι ὑπὲρ αὐτοῦ, ὅπως ἀναχωρή-
σῃ ἀπ᾽ αὐτοῦ τὸ ἀκάθαρτον πνεῦμα καὶ δοξάσῃ τὸν θεὸν
καὶ χρησιμεύσῃ ἐκ τοῦ πάθους αὐτοῦ.᾽ ὁ δὲ δοῦλος τοῦ
10 θεοῦ προσευξάμενος ἀπέλυσεν τοὺς δύο ἄνδρας καὶ

60. And in the following year they sowed the same piece of land, and they put in the same number of modii. And when the sowing was over, and the crops harvested from the land, they gathered one hundred and twenty-five large modii. And they gave thanks to God and to the prayer of the holy man Nicholas, for it was through it that they received such a blessing. The farmer John, recognizing that he had been deemed worthy of such a blessing through the prayers of the servant of God Nicholas, said to his wife: "Here, let us go and fall at the feet of the servant of God Nicholas, since through his holy prayer God deemed us worthy of such a great blessing." So they came to the servant of God Nicholas, and threw themselves at his feet, and after giving thanks they described all the wonders that had come to pass through his holy prayers, and how God had increased the produce of their land. And the servant of God said: "Go now, give thanks to God. For when God wishes He can increase what is small [in number] and diminish what is large." And he sent them away and they glorified God.

61. And a certain man by the name of Kosmas, who was a reader in the district of Eneanda, and [was] from the hamlet of Oualo, came to the Monastery of Holy Sion; he had un unclean spirit. And he was being escorted by two men, for he was out of his mind. And they fell before the servant of God Nicholas saying: "We beg you, venerable Father, have mercy on God's creature, and pray for him, that the unclean spirit may depart from him and he may glorify God and be [again] of use [once he is freed] from his affliction." The servant of God prayed, then sent

ἐκράτησεν τὸν ἀσθενοῦντα ἡμέρας τεσσαράκοντα. καὶ τῇ τοῦ θεοῦ φιλανθρωπίᾳ καὶ τῇ προσευχῇ τοῦ ὁσίου ἀνδρὸς μετὰ τὰς τεσσαράκοντα ἡμέρας ἀπέλυσεν αὐτὸν ὑγιῆ, δοξάζοντα καὶ αἰνοῦντα τὸν θεόν.

62. Καὶ μετὰ χρόνον ὀλίγον ἐκ τῆς αὐτῆς χώρας ἦλθεν ἄνθρωπος, ᾧ ὄνομα Παῦλος, ποιμὴν ὤν. καὶ ἐν τῷ ποιμνίῳ συνὼν εἰς τὸ ὄρος, ἐκρατήθη ὑπὸ ἀκαθάρτου πνεύματος. ἀκούσας δὲ παρὰ Κοσμᾶ τοῦ ἀναγνώστου τὴν
5 δύναμιν τῆς ἁγίας Σιὼν καὶ τὴν πίστιν τοῦ ὁσίου ἀνδρός, ἐλθὼν ἐν τῷ μοναστηρίῳ προσεκύνησεν αὐτὸν καὶ εἶπεν· 'Τίμιε πατὴρ καὶ δοῦλε τοῦ θεοῦ, ἐλευθέρωσον τὴν ἀθλίαν μου ψυχήν. δεήθητι οὖν τοῦ θεοῦ, ὅπως διὰ τῆς δεήσεώς σου τύχω κἀγὼ τῆς τοῦ θεοῦ φιλανθρωπίας ,
10 ὃν τρόπον Κοσμᾶς ὁ ἀναγνώστης, καὶ δοξάσω καὶ ἐγὼ ὁ ταπεινὸς τὰς ὁσίας σου εὐχάς.' καὶ σταθεὶς ὁ δοῦλος τοῦ θεοῦ Νικόλαος, κρατήσας αὐτὸν καὶ σφίγξας τῆς κεφαλῆς καὶ εὐξάμενος ἐπ' αὐτῷ, ἀπέλυσεν αὐτόν. καὶ
48Α ῥῆξαν αὐτὸν τὸ ἀκάθαρτον πνεῦμα ἐβόησεν· ''Ο δοῦλος
15 τοῦ θεοῦ Νικόλαος διώκει με, καὶ τί ποιήσω;' σταθεὶς δὲ ὁ δοῦλος τοῦ Θεοῦ ἐπάνω αὐτοῦ καὶ εὐξάμενος, ἀπέστησεν ἀπ' αὐτοῦ τὸ ἀκάθαρτον πνεῦμα. καὶ ἀνέστη ὑγιὴς ὁ ἄνθρωπος, καὶ προσεκύνησεν αὐτῷ δοξάζων τὸν θεόν, καὶ ἐπορεύθη εἰς τὸν οἶκον αὐτοῦ μετὰ σπουδῆς.

63. Ἐν μιᾷ δὲ τῶν ἡμερῶν ἦλθεν ἐκ τῆς Ἀρναβανδέων χώρας ἄνθρωπός τις ὀνόματι Ζήνων, καὶ αὐτὸς ἔχων πνεῦμα τοῦ δαιμονίου ἀκαθάρτου. καὶ ἦλθεν ἐν τῷ μοναστηρίῳ μετὰ ἄλλου ἑνὸς τοῦ ὁδηγοῦντος αὐτόν. ὁ δὲ δοῦ-
5 λος τοῦ θεοῦ Νικόλαος οὐκ ἦν ἐν τῷ μοναστηρίῳ, ἀλλὰ ἦν μετὰ τῶν ἀδελφῶν εἰς τὸ φυτεύειν τὸν ἀμπελῶνα. ἀκούσας δὲ ὁ ἄνθρωπος, ἐν ᾧ ἦν τὸ ἀκάθαρτον πνεῦμα,

the two men away, and kept the ailing man for forty days. And through God's love of mankind and the prayer of the holy man, after forty days Kosmas was sent away healed, and glorified and praised God.

62. And a short time later, there came a man from the same area: his name was Paul; he was a shepherd. And while he was with his flock on the mountain he became possessed by an unclean spirit. And since he had heard from the reader Kosmas of the power of Holy Sion and of the faith of the holy man, he came to the monastery, paid him reverence, and said: "O venerable Father and servant of God, make my wretched soul free. Entreat God, then, that through your entreaty I, too, may experience God's love toward men, the way Kosmas the reader did; and that I, too, the humble one, may bring glory to your holy prayers." And the servant of God Nicholas stood up and took hold of him and pressed his head and prayed over him and let him go. And that unclean spirit threw him down and cried out: "The servant of God Nicholas is persecuting me, and what shall I do?" The servant of God stood over him and prayed, and the unclean spirit departed from him. And the man arose healed, and reverenced Nicholas, and praised God and quickly journeyed home.

63. One day there came a man by the name of Zeno from the district of the Arnabandians; he, too, had a spirit of an unclean devil. And he came to the monastery with another man who escorted him. The servant of God Nicholas was not in the monastery, but was with the brethren planting the vineyard. When the man possessed by the unclean spirit heard this, he went down to the place

ἀπῆλθεν πρὸς τὸν δοῦλον τοῦ θεοῦ Νικόλαον, ὅπου ἦν
κάμνων, καὶ προσεκύνησεν αὐτόν. καὶ κρατήσας καὶ
10 σφραγίσας αὐτὸν τῇ δυνάμει τοῦ ἁγίου πνεύματος, ἐπέδωκεν αὐτῷ *τὸ δικέλλιν* καὶ ἐπέταξεν αὐτῷ κάμνειν. καὶ
αὐτῇ τῇ ὥρᾳ σωφρονήσας ὁ ἄνθρωπος ἐδόξασεν τὸν
θεὸν καὶ ἔκαμνεν. ἦν δὲ ἡ ὥρα ἐνάτη τῆς προσευχῆς.

64. Καὶ μετὰ ἡμέρας τινὰς ἦλθαν συνοδία ἐκ τῆς Σεροι-
ατέων κώμης, φέροντες ἄνθρωπον ὀνόματι Παῦλον, ὄντα ἀναγνώστην, ἔχοντα πνεῦμα πονηρόν· ὃς ἦν νενεκρω-
μένος καὶ ἐβαστάζετο. καὶ ἐλθόντες ἔρριψαν αὐτὸν εἰς
5 τοὺς πόδας τοῦ δούλου τοῦ θεοῦ Νικολάου, λέγοντες·
'Ὅσιε πατήρ, ἐλέησον τὸ πλάσμα τοῦ θεοῦ.' ἰδὼν δὲ
αὐτὸν ὁ τοῦ θεοῦ δοῦλος Νικόλαος, εὐξάμενος ἐπ'
αὐτῷ—ἐφυγαδεύθη τὸ πνεῦμα τὸ ἀκάθαρτον. καὶ σωφρονήσας καὶ παραμένων τῇ ἁγίᾳ Σιών, ἐποίει τὴν τάξιν
10 τοῦ ἀναγνώστου εἰς τὸν ὄρθρον καὶ εἰς τὰ ἑσπερινά, καὶ
ἔψαλλεν καὶ ἀνεγίνωσκεν εὐχαριστῶν τῷ θεῷ. καὶ ἐπορεύθη εἰς τὸν οἶκον αὐτοῦ ὑγιής.

65. Καὶ μεθ' ἡμέρας τινὰς ἐκ τῆς αὐτῆς κώμης Σεροια-
τέων ἦλθέν τις ὀνόματι Κυριακός, κἀκεῖνος ἔχων πνεῦμα
49Α   πονηρόν. καὶ ἰδὼν τὸν δοῦλον τοῦ θεοῦ Νικόλαον, ἔπε-
σεν εἰς τοὺς πόδας αὐτοῦ, παρακαλῶν αὐτὸν καὶ λέγων·
5 'Ὅσιε τοῦ θεοῦ πατήρ, εὖξαι καὶ ἐπ' ἐμοὶ τῷ ἁμαρτωλῷ,
ὡς ἐπὶ πᾶσιν, ἵνα διὰ τῆς προσευχῆς σου λυτρωθῶ ἐκ
τῆς παγίδος τοῦ διαβόλου καὶ δοξάσω τὸν θεὸν καὶ τὴν
σὴν ἁγιωσύνην.' καὶ σταθεὶς ὁ τοῦ θεοῦ δοῦλος Νικόλαος καὶ ἐπευξάμενος αὐτῷ, ἐφυγάδευσεν τὸ ἀκάθαρ-
10 τον πνεῦμα, καὶ διὰ τριάκοντα ἡμερῶν ἀπέλυσεν αὐτὸν
εὐχαριστοῦντα καὶ αἰνοῦντα τὸν θεόν.

where the servant of God Nicholas was working, and reverenced him. And Nicholas took hold of him, blessed him with the sign of the cross by the power of the Holy Spirit, gave him the hoe and bade him to work. And at that very moment the man regained his senses, praised God and went on working. It was the ninth hour of prayer.

64. And some days later there came a party from the village of the Seroiatians, with a man by the name of Paul, who was a reader, and who had an evil spirit. He was as good as dead and was being carried. And they came and cast him down at the feet of the servant of God Nicholas, saying: "O holy Father, have mercy on God's creature." When the servant of God saw him, he prayed over him and the unclean spirit was put to flight. And Paul regained his senses and, remaining at Holy Sion, performed the functions of reader at Matins and Vespers, and sang Psalms and recited the readings, giving thanks to God. And he journeyed to his home healed.

65. And some days later there came a certain man by the name of Kyriakos, from the same village of the Seroiatians; he, too, had an evil spirit. And when he saw the servant of God Nicholas, he fell at his feet, beseeching him, and saying: "O Father, holy man of God, pray for me the sinner, too, as you do for them all, so that through your prayer I may be released from the devil's snare, and may glorify God and Your Holiness." And the servant of God Nicholas stood and prayed over him, and drove away the unclean spirit, and after thirty days he sent him away, thanking and praising God.

66. Μιᾷ δὲ τῶν ἡμερῶν ἦλθεν ἄνθρωπος μετὰ τοῦ πατρὸς
αὐτοῦ ἀπὸ τῆς κώμης τοῦ Πληνίου, ἀπὸ χωρίου Ραββα-
μουσᾶ οὕτω καλουμένου. καὶ τὸ ὄνομα τοῦ ἀσθενοῦντος Ἑρμῆς, ἔχων πνεῦμα πονηρόν. καὶ πεσὼν εἰς τοὺς
5 πόδας αὐτοῦ παρεκάλει τὸν ὅσιον εὔξασθαι ὑπὲρ αὐτοῦ.
καὶ σφραγίσας αὐτὸν ὁ δοῦλος τοῦ θεοῦ Νικόλαος, ἀπέλυσεν αὐτὸν διὰ δέκα πέντε ἡμερῶν. καὶ ἀπῆλθεν εἰς
τὸν οἶκον αὐτοῦ ὑγιής, δοξάζων τὸν θεόν.

67. Μετὰ δὲ τὴν προγραφεῖσαν καὶ προτελεσθεῖσαν πᾶσαν τοῦ ἁγίου πνεύματος δωρεάν, πνεῦμα ἅγιον φαίνεται κατ᾽ ὄναρ τῷ προλεχθέντι ὁσίῳ Νικολάῳ, ἐπιδεικνύων αὐτῷ θρόνον ἔνδοξον καὶ σχῆμα τῆς ἱερωσύνης,
5 κελεύων αὐτῷ καθεσθῆναι ἐπὶ τοῦ θρόνου καὶ ἐπιδεικνύων αὐτῷ θυσιαστήριον δόξης. καὶ διυπνισθεὶς ὁ τοῦ
θεοῦ δοῦλος Νικόλαος διελογίζετο ἐν ἑαυτῷ, λέγων· ᾽τίς
ἂν εἴη ἡ τοιαύτη ὀπτασία;᾽ καὶ ἀναστὰς αὐτῇ τῇ ὥρᾳ,
ἔστη ἐν τῇ προσευχῇ ἐν τῷ εὐκτηρίῳ τοῦ εὐαγοῦς αὐτοῦ
10 μοναστηρίου. καὶ ἐπὶ πλεῖον ἐν ἀγῶνι γενάμενος περὶ
τῆς ἐπιστάσης αὐτῷ ἐπισκιάσεως, καὶ ἐφύλαττεν τὸ ὅρα-
μα διὰ παντός, μηδενὶ ἐξηγησάμενος, ἕως ὅτου ἔφθασεν αὐτὸν ἡ τοιαύτη ἔνδοξος ἐπιστασία καὶ τοῦ θεοῦ
εὐλογία.

68. Μετὰ δὲ μῆνας τρεῖς δηλοῖ αὐτῷ Φίλιππος, ὁ ὁσιώτατος ἀρχιεπίσκοπος τῆς Μυρέων μητροπόλεως, ἐπὶ τὸ
50Α κατελθεῖν αὐτὸν ἐν τῷ ἐπισκοπείῳ. ἦν δὲ σάββατον τῶν
ἡμερῶν. καὶ τῇ ἐπιούσῃ ἁγίᾳ κυριακῇ ἐφανέρωσεν αὐτῷ
5 ὁ ὁσιώτατος ἀρχιεπίσκοπος ἐπὶ τὸ χειροτονῆσαι αὐτὸν
ἐπίσκοπον. τῇ οὖν εἰσόδῳ τῆς συνάξεως τῆς ἁγίας τοῦ

66. One day there came a man with his father from the village of Plenion, from the hamlet called Rhabbamousa. And the name of the sick man was Hermes; he had an evil spirit. And he fell down at Nicholas' feet and besought the holy man to pray for him. And the servant of God Nicholas made the sign of the cross over him and sent him away after fifteen days. And he departed to his home healed, glorifying God.

67. After all these gifts of the Holy Spirit, previously granted and described above, the Holy Spirit appeared to the aforesaid holy Nicholas in a dream, pointing to a seat of honor and a garb of priesthood, bidding him to be seated in that seat, and showing him an altar of glory. And the servant of God Nicholas awoke and debated within himself, saying: "What might such a vision mean?" And rising at that moment, he stood in prayer in the shrine of his venerable monastery. And he grew more and more anxious about the overshadowing that had come upon him, and he kept the dream [to himself] all the time, explaining it to no one, not until such a glorious overseer's office and God's blessing came upon him.

68. Three months later, Philip, the most holy archbishop of the metropolis of Myra, sent word to him that he should come down to the episcopal residence. The day was Saturday. And on the following holy Sunday, the most holy archbishop revealed to him that he would ordain him

θεοῦ καθολικῆς καὶ ἀποστολικῆς ἐκκλησίας Εἰρήνης
παρέσχεν αὐτῷ τὸ σχῆμα τῆς ἱερωσύνης, καὶ ἐκήρυξεν
αὐτὸν ἐπίσκοπον τῆς Πιναρέων πόλεως, καὶ ἐξέπεμψεν
10 αὐτὸν εἰς τὴν προλεχθεῖσαν πόλιν. καὶ πάντες ἐθαύμα-
σαν τὰ περὶ τοῦ ὁσίου ἀνδρὸς Νικολάου, πῶς ἐδόξασεν αὐτὸν ὁ θεός.

69. Μετὰ δὲ τὸν ἐνθρονιασμὸν αὐτοῦ ὡς μετὰ χρόνους
τρεῖς φαίνεται αὐτῷ ἡ ἔνδοξος καὶ ἀειπάρθενος καὶ μήτηρ τοῦ κυρίου ἡμῶν Ἰησοῦ Χριστοῦ, ἐπιδεικνύουσα
αὐτῷ τόπον καὶ μέτρα εὐκτηρίου τῆς ἰδίας ὀνομασίας,
5 ἐπὶ τὸ ἐξεγεῖραι τὸν ναὸν τῆς ἁγίας Μαρίας. καὶ ἀναστὰς
καὶ παραγενόμενος ἐν τῷ τόπῳ, ὃν ἔδειξεν αὐτῷ ἡ ἔνδοξος μήτηρ τοῦ Χριστοῦ, καταμετρεῖ τὸν τόπον. γνόν-
τες δὲ οἱ ἐκεῖσε οἰκοῦντες πολιτευόμενοι, ἀντεπάθησαν
σὺν τοῖς κληρικοῖς, καὶ διεκώλυον αὐτὸν τοῦ μὴ κτίσαι
10 καὶ πληρῶσαι τὴν τοῦ θεοῦ ὀπτασίαν. τοῦ δὲ ἁγίου πνεύματος μὴ συγχωροῦντος, ἀλλ᾽ ἐνδυναμοῦντος τὸν τοῦ
θεοῦ δοῦλον Νικόλαον, βίᾳ φιλονεικήσας καὶ μὴ συγ-
χωρήσας μήτε συγχωρούμενος κτίσαι, ἠναγκάσθη ἀγο-
ράσαι τὸν ἐπιδειχθέντα αὐτῷ ἅγιον τόπον. καὶ τότε ἀρ-
15 ξάμενος ἔκτισεν καὶ ἐπλήρωσεν καὶ ἠνέῳξεν τὸν ἔνδοξον τῆς Θεοτόκου ἅγιον οἶκον. καὶ εὐχαριστήσας τῷ θεῷ
ἦλθεν εἰς τὸ εὐαγὲς αὐτοῦ καὶ ἔνδοξον μοναστήριον. καὶ
ψηφίσας τὴν ἔκβασιν τοῦ κτίσματος τοῦ ἁγίου οἴκου τῆς
Θεοτόκου, ηὑρέθησαν νομίσματα τετρακόσια.

70. Καὶ μετ᾽ ὀλίγας ἡμέρας κατέρχεται ὁ τοῦ θεοῦ δοῦλος
εἰς τὸν ἅγιον οἶκον τοῦ ἀρχαγγέλου εἰς Κροβᾶ. καί τις
γυνὴ ἀπὸ τοῦ χωρίου Κυπαρίσσου εἶχεν υἱόν, ὃς ὠχλεῖτο
ὑπὸ ῥυπαροῦ καὶ ἀκαθάρτου δαίμονος καὶ ἔτρωγεν τὰ
5 ἱμάτια, ἃ ἐφόρει. καὶ προσήνεγκεν αὐτὸν ἡ μήτηρ αὐτοῦ

bishop. So during the Entrance of the service held in God's holy cathedral and apostolic church of [God's] Peace, he endowed him with the garb of priesthood, proclaimed him bishop of the city of Pinara, and sent him to the aforesaid city. And everyone marvelled over the holy man Nicholas, how God had glorified him.

69. Some three years after his accession, the glorious and Ever-virgin and Mother of our Lord Jesus Christ appeared to him, indicating to him the emplacement and measurements of a shrine to be named after herself, that he might erect the Church of Holy Mary. And he arose, reached the spot which the glorious Mother of Christ had shown him, and measured off that spot. When the magistrates living there learned about this, they opposed [him], together with the clergy, and attempted to prevent him from doing the building and fulfilling [the terms of] the Godly vision. But as the Holy Spirit did not allow it to happen, but rather gave strength to the servant of God Nicholas, after vigorous litigation, Nicholas neither yielded [to them] nor was allowed to build, and was obliged to purchase the hallowed spot that had been indicated to him. Beginning then, he built, completed, and inaugurated the glorious holy shrine of the Theotokos. And giving thanks to God he went to his venerable and glorious monastery. And when he added up the [cost of] completing and building the holy shrine of the Theotokos, it came to four hundred nomismata.

70. And a few days later the servant of God went down to the holy shrine of the Archangel in Kroba. And a certain woman from the hamlet of Kyparissos had a son who was vexed with a foul and unclean demon and chewed the clothes which he wore. And his mother brought him to the

51A τῷ δούλῳ τοῦ θεοῦ. καὶ κρατήσας αὐτὸν ὁ τοῦ θεοῦ δοῦλος ἐνεφύσησεν αὐτῷ εἰς τὸ στόμα. καὶ τῇ τοῦ θεοῦ δυνάμει ἐκαθαρίσθη, καὶ οὐκέτι ἐποίησέν τι πονηρόν. καὶ ἐδόξασαν οἱ γονεῖς αὐτοῦ τὸν θεὸν καὶ τὴν πίστιν τοῦ ὁσίου.

71. Καὶ πάλιν ἐν μιᾷ τῶν ἡμερῶν γυνή τις ἀπὸ τοῦ χωρίου
Νικάπω, οὖσα ξηρὰ ἀπὸ ἀκαθάρτου πνεύματος—
ἐβάστασεν αὐτὴν ὁ ἀνὴρ αὐτῆς, καὶ ἤνεγκεν εἰς τὸ μοναστήριον, καὶ ἔρριψεν εἰς τοὺς πόδας τοῦ ὁσίου. ὁ δὲ δοῦ-
5 λος τοῦ θεοῦ ηὔξατο πρὸς τὸν θεόν, καὶ ἀνεχώρησεν ἀπ᾽
αὐτῆς τὸ πονηρὸν πνεῦμα, καὶ ἰάθη. καὶ ἀπὸ τῆς ὥρας
ἐκείνης ἰδίοις ποσὶν ἀπῆλθεν εἰς τὸν οἶκον αὐτῆς, εὐχαριστοῦσα τῷ θεῷ καὶ τῇ ἁγίᾳ Σιών.

72. Ἦν δὲ ὁ καιρὸς τῶν ἁγίων νηστειῶν, καὶ ἔρχεται
ἄνθρωπος καθήμενος ζῶον, ἦν γὰρ ξηρός, ᾧ ὄνομα Νικόλαος, ἐκ τῆς κώμης τοῦ Σιβινοῦ. καὶ προσπίπτουσιν
ἐν τῇ ἁγίᾳ Σιὼν καὶ τῷ δούλῳ τοῦ θεοῦ Νικολάῳ, τῷ
5 θεοφιλεστάτῳ ἀρχιεπισκόπῳ, λέγοντες· ᾽Δοῦλε τοῦ
θεοῦ, εὖξαι ὑπὲρ τοῦ ταπεινοῦ τούτου, ὅπως ὁσίαις ὑμῶν
εὐχαῖς σπλαγχνισθῇ ἐπ᾽ αὐτῷ ὁ θεός.᾽ ὁ δὲ δοῦλος τοῦ
θεοῦ Νικόλαος σφραγίσας αὐτὸν ἐκ τῆς δεσποτικῆς
κανδήλας καὶ ἐπευξάμενος, δι᾽ ὀλίγων ἡμερῶν ἀπεκατέ-
10 στη ὑγιής, καὶ ἀπῆλθεν εἰς τὸν οἶκον αὐτοῦ δοξάζων τὸν
θεόν.

73. Καὶ πάλιν ἦλθεν ἄνθρωπος ἐν τῷ μοναστηρίῳ τῆς
ἁγίας Σιὼν πρὸς τὸν δοῦλον τοῦ θεοῦ Νικόλαον, ὀνόματι
Τιμόθεος, ἐκ τῆς κώμης Κενδήμων, ὃς εἶχεν πνεῦμα πο-
νηρόν· καὶ ἐκ τοῦ πνεύματος τύπτων τὴν κεφαλήν, εἶχεν
5 σκώληκας ἡ κεφαλὴ αὐτοῦ. ἦλθεν δὲ κατεχόμενος ὑπὸ

104

servant of God. And God's servant took hold of him, and breathed into his mouth. And by the power of God he was cleansed, and no longer did anything harmful. And his parents glorified God and the faith of the holy man.

71. And again, one day, [there came] a certain woman from the hamlet of Nikapo who was withered from the unclean spirit, and her husband carried her and brought her to the monastery, and he cast her down at the feet of the holy man. The servant of God prayed to God, and the evil spirit withdrew from her, and she was made whole. And from that very hour she went home on her own feet giving thanks to God and to Holy Sion.

72. It was the time of the Holy Fast and there came a man from the village of Sibinos by the name of Nicholas; he was riding on an animal, for he was withered. And they [*sic*] fell down before Holy Sion and the servant of God Nicholas, the bishop most beloved of God, saying: "O servant of God, pray for this humble man, that through your holy prayers God may be moved with compassion for him." The servant of God Nicholas made the sign of the cross over him [with oil] from the lamp of the Lord, and prayed, and a few days later the man was restored whole, and departed to his own house, glorifying God.

73. And again, a man by the name of Timothy, from the village of Kendemoi, came to the Monastery of Holy Sion to the servant of God Nicholas; he had an evil spirit. And since he beat his head because of the spirit, his head had worms. He came held down by three men. And they came

τριῶν, καὶ ἐλθόντες προσεκύνησαν τὴν ἁγίαν Σιὼν καὶ
τὸν θεοφιλέστατον ἄνδρα, λέγοντες· 'Δοῦλε τοῦ θεοῦ,
ἴδε τὴν θλῖψιν τοῦ ἀνθρώπου τούτου καὶ εὖξαι τῷ θεῷ,
ὅπως διὰ τῆς προσευχῆς σου ἐλεηθῇ.' *καὶ σφραγίσας*
10 *αὐτόν, ἔλαβεν* ἔλαιον ἐκ τῆς δεσποτικῆς κανδήλας· καὶ
τῇ τοῦ θεοῦ δυνάμει δι' ὀλίγων ἡμερῶν ὑγιὴς ἀπελύθη
ἀπὸ τῶν ὁσίων αὐτοῦ χειρῶν, καὶ ἀπῆλθεν εἰς τὸν οἶκον
αὐτοῦ εὐλογῶν τὸν θεόν.

52Α 74. Ἐν δὲ ταῖς ἡμέραις ἐκείναις ἦλθεν ἄνθρωπος ἐν τῷ
μοναστηρίῳ ὀνόματι Λέων, ἐκ τῆς κώμης Ἀρναβανδῶν,
ἔχων πνεῦμα ἀκάθαρτον καὶ κρατούμενος ὑπὸ τριῶν,
περιεσχισμένος, διαρρήξας καὶ ὃ ἦν διεζωσμένος. καὶ
5 προσκυνήσαντες τῷ ὁσίῳ, λέγουσιν αὐτῷ· 'Δοῦλε τοῦ
θεοῦ, εὖξαι ὑπὲρ τοῦ ἀθλίου τούτου.' καὶ λαβὼν ἔλαιον
ἐκ τῆς κανδήλας, ἐσφράγισεν αὐτόν. καὶ διὰ τεσσαράκοντα ἡμερῶν ἀπῆλθεν εἰς τὸν οἶκον αὐτοῦ αἰνῶν τὸν
θεόν.

75. Καί τις γυνὴ ἀπὸ Ἐδρασῶν ἦλθεν μετὰ τοῦ ἀνδρὸς
αὐτῆς, θέλουσα προσκυνῆσαι τὸν δοῦλον τοῦ θεοῦ καὶ
παρακαλέσαι αὐτὸν εὔξασθαι ὑπὲρ αὐτῆς, ἵνα δῴη αὐτῇ
ὁ θεὸς τέκνον· ὅτι εἴκοσιν ὀκτὼ ἔτη εἶχεν μετὰ τοῦ
5 ἀνδρὸς αὐτῆς, καὶ τέκνον οὐκ ἐποίει. ὁ δὲ δοῦλος τοῦ
θεοῦ ἦν ἐν Μύροις τῇ μητροπόλει. καὶ περιέμειναν ἐν
τῷ μοναστηρίῳ ἡμέρας τρεῖς. ἔτι δὲ βραδύνοντος τοῦ
δούλου τοῦ θεοῦ ἐν Μύροις, ἠναγκάσθησαν κατελθεῖν
ἐν Μύροις, πιστεύσαντες τῷ θεῷ καὶ προσκυνήσαντες
10 αὐτῷ. ἀπερχομένων δὲ αὐτῶν, συνήντησεν αὐτοῖς ὁ δοῦλος τοῦ θεοῦ ἐν τῷ ἀνάβῳ, ἐρχόμενος εἰς τὸν καλούμε-
νον Στρατιώτην. καὶ προσκυνήσαντες αὐτῷ ἐξηγήσαντο
αὐτῷ πάντα. καὶ εὐξάμενος καὶ κατασφραγίσας αὐτοὺς
εἶπεν· ''Υπάγετε, πιστεύσατε εἰς τὸν θεὸν καὶ εἰς τὴν
15 ἁγίαν Σιών, καὶ δοῦναι ὑμῖν ἔχει ὁ θεὸς καρπὸν

and reverenced Holy Sion and the man most beloved of God, saying: "O servant of God, behold the affliction of this man, and pray to God that through your prayer he will find mercy." And he took oil from the lamp of the Lord, and made the sign of the cross over him; and by the power of God, a few days later the man was released from his holy hands healed, and departed to his own house, praising God.

74. In those days a man by the name of Leo, from the village of Arnabanda, came to the monastery; he had an unclean spirit. And he was held by three men, stripped of his clothes, having ripped apart even what was girdling him. And they reverenced the holy man, saying to him: "O servant of God, pray for this wretch." And he took oil from the lamp, and made the sign of the cross over him. And forty days later the man departed to his own house, praising God.

75. And a certain woman from Edrasa came with her husband, wishing to reverence the servant of God, and beseech him to pray for her, that God might give her a child. For she had spent twenty-eight years with her husband, and could not produce a child. The servant of God was in the metropolis of Myra. And they waited in the monastery for three days. As the servant of God still tarried in Myra, they were obliged to go down to Myra, having shown faith in God and reverenced Him. They started off, and the servant of God met them on his way up [?] coming to the so-called Stratiotes. And they reverenced him and explained everything to him. And he made the sign of the cross over them, and said: "Go now, have faith in God and Holy Sion, and God will give you a male offspring. I myself,

ἀρρενικόν· καὶ ἐγώ, ἁμαρτωλὸς ὤν, γίνομαι ἀνάδοχος.'
καὶ προσκυνήσαντες αὐτόν, ἀνεχώρησαν εἰς τὰ ἴδια. καὶ
εἰς τὸ ἐπιὸν ἔτος τῆς τοῦ ἁγίου Πάσχα ἑορτῆς ἦλθον
προσκυνῆσαι τὴν ἁγίαν Σιὼν μετὰ ἀρρενικοῦ παιδίου.
20 καὶ εὐλογήσας αὐτοὺς ὁ θεοφιλέστατος δοῦλος τοῦ θεοῦ
Νικόλαος, ἐφώτισεν τὸ παιδίον καὶ ἐδέξατο αὐτούς, με-
γάλως εὐλογήσας, καὶ ἀπέλυσεν αὐτούς.

76. Φθάσαντος δὲ τοῦ καιροῦ τῶν Ῥοσσαλίων τοῦ προ-
πάτορος ἡμῶν τοῦ ἁγίου Νικολάου, κατῆλθεν ἐν Μύροις
τῇ μητροπόλει εἰς τὴν σύνοδον ὁ τοῦ θεοῦ δοῦλος Νικόλαος. καὶ εὐξάμενος, καὶ ἀπολαύσας τῶν ἁγίων καὶ τῶν
5 τιμίων πατέρων καὶ συλλειτουργῶν τῆς ἐν Χριστῷ ἁγίας
συνόδου, καὶ ἀσπασάμενος πάντας καὶ τὴν εἰρήνην
πᾶσιν ἀποδεδωκώς, ἀνῆλθεν εἰς τὸ εὐαγὲς αὐτοῦ μοναστήριον, καὶ συνελήφθη ἐν ἀρρωστίᾳ.

53Α **77.** Κατακειμένου δὲ αὐτοῦ καὶ ἀσθενοῦντος, ἦλθέν τις
γυνὴ ὀνόματι Εὐγένεια, ἐκ τῆς κώμης Σοκλῶν, ἔχουσα
πνεῦμα σεληνιακόν. καὶ προσπεσοῦσα αὐτῷ, κατεσφρά-
γισεν αὐτήν. καὶ εὐξάμενος ἐπ᾽ αὐτῇ, κατακείμενος ἐν
5 τῇ κλίνῃ καὶ μέλλων παραδιδόναι τὴν παραθήκην, ὁ τοῦ
θεοῦ δοῦλος Νικόλαος ἐθεράπευσεν αὐτήν. ἡ δὲ γυνὴ ἡ
ἰαθεῖσα παρέμενεν ἐν τῇ ἁγίᾳ Σιών, εὐχαριστοῦσα τῷ
θεῷ.

78. Ὅτε δὲ εἶδεν ὁ ὁσιώτατος καὶ μακαριώτατος *καὶ*
δοῦλος τοῦ θεοῦ Νικόλαος τὸ ἀπαραίτητον πρόσταγμα
τοῦ θανάτου, ἤρξατο εὔχεσθαι καὶ ψάλλειν καὶ παρακα-
λεῖν τὸν θεὸν ἐπὶ τὸ ἀγαθὴν προσταγὴν κελεῦσαι τῇ τῶν
5 ἀποστελλομένων αὐτῷ ἁγίων ἀγγέλων ⟨ τάξει ⟩, τοῦ δέ-

108

though a sinner, will be his godfather.'' And they reverenced him and went back home. And the following year, on the feast of Holy Easter, they came to reverence Holy Sion with a male child. And the servant of God Nicholas, most beloved of God, blessed them, baptized the child, entertained them, bestowed generous blessings upon them, and sent them away.

76. When the time of the Rossalia of our forefather Saint Nicholas came, the servant of God Nicholas went down to the metropolis of Myra, to take part in the Synod. And he prayed, and, having enjoyed the [company of] the holy men [?] and of the venerable fathers, who were his concelebrants at the holy Synod in Christ, he embraced them all, gave [the kiss of] peace to all, went back up to his venerable monastery, and was seized by illness.

77. While he was bedridden and ailing, there came a certain woman by the name of Eugeneia, from the village of Sokla, who had a spirit of lunacy. And she fell down before him, and he made the sign of the cross over her. And having prayed over her, bedridden as he was and about to hand over that which had been committed to him [that is, his soul], the servant of God Nicholas healed her. And the woman who was cured stayed in Holy Sion, giving thanks to God.

78. When the most holy and most blessed servant of God Nicholas beheld the inexorable decree of death, he began to pray and to sing Psalms and to beseech God that He give favorable orders to the [host of] angels that were be-

ξασθαι ἀπ᾽ αὐτοῦ τὴν παραθήκην. καὶ θεασάμενος τοὺς
ἐνδόξους προστάτας καὶ πρεσβευτάς, τοὺς ἁγίους ἀγγέ-
λους, ἐρχομένους ἐπ᾽ αὐτόν, κλίνας τὴν κεφαλὴν καὶ
σφραγίσας ἑαυτὸν εἰς ὄνομα πατρὸς καὶ υἱοῦ καὶ ἁγίου
10 πνεύματος, προσεκύνησεν καὶ εἶπεν· '«Ἐπὶ σοί, κύριε,
ἤλπισα· μὴ καταισχυνθείην εἰς τὸν αἰῶνα. ἐν τῇ δικαι-
οσύνῃ σου ῥῦσαί με καὶ ἐξελοῦ με,»' καὶ τὰ ἑξῆς, ἕως
'«κύριε, εἰς χεῖράς σου παραθήσομαι τὸ πνεῦμά μου.»'
καὶ πληρώσας τὴν προσευχήν, μετὰ δόξης παρέδωκεν
15 τὸ πνεῦμα, εὐλογήσας τὸν θεόν· παρισταμένων αὐτῷ τῶν
γνησίων αὐτοῦ ἀδελφῶν, ‹ Ἑρμαίου καὶ › Ἀρτεμᾶ τοῦ
54A εὐλαβεστάτου πρεσβυτέρου [καὶ Νικολάου τοῦ θεοφιλεστάτου ἀρχιδιακόνου] καὶ ὑπουργοῦ ἤτοι δευτεραρίου
αὐτοῦ· ὃν καὶ περιπτυξάμενος ἐν τῷ τραχήλῳ, ἀφῆκεν
20 τὴν ψυχὴν εἰς χεῖρας τῶν ὀφθέντων αὐτῷ ἁγίων ἀρχαγ-
γέλων ἐν εἰρήνῃ. Νικόλαος δὲ ὁ εὐλαβέστατος ἀρχιδιά-
κονος συνέστειλεν τὸ ἅγιον αὐτοῦ λείψανον, καὶ τὴν
κόρην τῶν ὀμμάτων καὶ τὴν ἔνδοξον †στήλην† τοῦ προ-
σώπου ἔσφιγξεν, ἅμα Ἀρτεμᾶ τῷ εὐλαβεστάτῳ πρεσβυ-
25 τέρῳ καὶ ἀρχιμανδρίτῃ, παρισταμένου καὶ Νικολάου
διακόνου καὶ κελλαρίου καὶ πάντων τῶν ἀδελφῶν τῶν
οἰκούντων ἐν τῷ εὐαγεῖ αὐτοῦ μοναστηρίῳ.

79. Καὶ γεναμένης θλίψεως, κραυγῆς τε καὶ ὀδυρμοῦ καὶ
πένθους μεγάλου, ἔφθασεν Παῦλος Ἑρμαίου ὁ εὐλαβέστατος διάκονος ὁ ἀπὸ τοῦ χωρίου Οὐμβῆ εἰς τὸ αὐτὸ
ἔνδοξον αὐτὸς θρῆνος. καὶ παραμυθησάμενος πάντας
5 τοὺς ὁσίους πατέρας καὶ ἀδελφούς, αὐτὸς κατέβη ἐν
Μύροις εἰς ἀπάντησιν Φιλίππου, τοῦ θεοφιλεστάτου ἐπισκόπου τῆς Φελλιτῶν πόλεως, ἐπὶ τὸ κηδεῦσαι αὐτόν.
καὶ ἀνελθὼν ὁ προλεχθεὶς θεοφιλέστατος ἐπίσκοπος,
ἐτέλεσεν τὰς ψαλμῳδίας καὶ τὰς ἀναγνώσεις, καθὼς
10 συνέταξαν οἱ ἅγιοι πατέρες ἐν τοῖς κανόσιν.

ing sent to him to receive his soul from him. And beholding
the holy angels, these glorious protectors and intercessors, coming toward him, he bowed his head and crossed himself in the
name of the Father and the Son and the Holy Spirit, and pro-
strated himself and said: " 'In Thee, O Lord, do I put my trust;
let me never be ashamed. Deliver me in Thy righteousness and
rescue me,' " and so on until " 'Lord, into Thine hands I will
commit my spirit.' " And when he finished the prayer, he gave
up the ghost with glory, having given praise to God. And at
his side were his very own brothers, [Hermaios and] Artemas
the most devout priest, [who also was] his assistant, that is,
deuterarios. And having embraced him, he yielded up his soul
in peace into the hands of the holy archangels who had appeared to him. Nicholas the most devout archdeacon shroud-
ed his holy remains and [closed] his eyelids and tied the
honorable base [?] of his face, along with Artemas the most
devout priest and archimandrite. Also present were Nicholas
the deacon and cellarer and all the brethren living in his
venerable monastery.

79. And there were grief and wailing and lamentation and great
mourning. And Paul [son] of Hermaios, the most devout
deacon from the hamlet of Oumbe, arrived himself [?] for that
[?] honorable wake. Having consoled all the holy fathers and
brethren, he went down to Myra to meet Philip, God's most
beloved bishop of the city of the Phellites, that Philip might
bury Nicholas. And the aforementioned bishop, most beloved
of God, came up and performed the psalmody and readings,
as the holy fathers have appointed it in the Canons.

80. Ἐτελειώθη δὲ ὁ τοῦ θεοῦ δοῦλος καὶ ὁσιώτατος ἐπίσκοπος Νικόλαος κατὰ τὴν τοῦ θεοῦ φιλανθρωπίαν μηνὶ
55A Δεκεμβρίῳ δεκάτῃ, ἡμέρᾳ τετάρτῃ, ἰνδικτιῶνος τρισκαι-
δεκάτης, ἐπὶ βασιλείας τοῦ φιλοχρίστου ἡμῶν βασιλέως
5 Ἰουστινιανοῦ ἔτους τριακοστοῦ καὶ ὀγδόου, ἐπὶ τοῦ ὁσι-
ωτάτου ἀρχιεπισκόπου * * * καὶ πατριάρχου *Μακαρίου*.
καὶ κατετέθη τὸ ἅγιον καὶ θεοφιλὲς αὐτοῦ λείψανον ἔνδον τῆς ἁγίας καὶ ἐνδόξου Σιών, ἔνθα τὰ λείψανα ἀπό-
κεινται τῶν ἐνδόξων, ἀθλοφόρων καὶ καλλινίκων
10 ἁγίων μαρτύρων, τοῦ ἁγίου Ἰωάννου τοῦ προδρόμου καὶ
βαπτιστοῦ καὶ τοῦ ἁγίου Στεφάνου τοῦ πρωτομάρτυρος
καὶ τοῦ ἁγίου Θεοδώρου καὶ τῶν ἁγίων Σεργίου καὶ Βάκ-
χου καὶ τῶν ἁγίων τεσσαράκοντα· ἐν τῷ δεξιῷ γυναικί-
τῃ δεξιᾷ κατασταθείς. ἐπλήρωσεν τὸν βίον καὶ πρεσβεύει
15 ὑπὲρ πάντων τῶν πιστευόντων εἰς τὸ ὄνομα τοῦ πατρὸς
καὶ τοῦ υἱοῦ καὶ τοῦ ἁγίου πνεύματος, ὡς πάντοτε, καὶ
νῦν καὶ ἀεὶ καὶ εἰς τοὺς αἰῶνας τῶν αἰώνων. ἀμήν.

80   The servant of God and most holy Bishop Nicholas died, by [the will of] God, Lover of mankind, on Wednesday, the tenth of the month of December, in the thirteenth Indiction, in the thirty-eighth year of the rule of our God-loving Emperor Justinian, at the time of the most holy Archbishop ∗ ∗ ∗ and of Patriarch Makarios. And his holy remains, beloved of God, were buried inside Holy and glorious Sion, where are deposited the remains of the glorious, victorious, triumphant, and holy martyrs, Saint John the Forerunner and Baptist, Saint Stephen the Protomartyr, and Saint Theodore, and Saints Sergios and Bakchos and the Holy Forty [Martyrs]. He was buried in the right part of the right section for women. He fulfilled his life, and is interceding for all who believe in the name of the Father and the Son and the Holy Spirit, as always, so now and forever and to the ages of ages. Amen.

PLATES

1. The Birth of St. Nicholas. Detail from an icon of St. Nicholas, Mount Sinai, St. Catherine's Monastery. Late twelfth century

2. The Schooling of St. Nicholas. Detail from an icon of St. Nicholas, Patmos, Monastery of St. John the Theologian. Fifteenth century

3. St. Nicholas fells the cypress of Plakoma. Agoriane, Church of St. Nicholas.
Late thirteenth century

4. St. Nicholas fells the cypress of Plakoma. Staro Nagoričane,
Church of St. George. Early fourteenth century

5. Sea scene with devils. Staro Nagoričane, Church of St. George.
Early fourteenth century

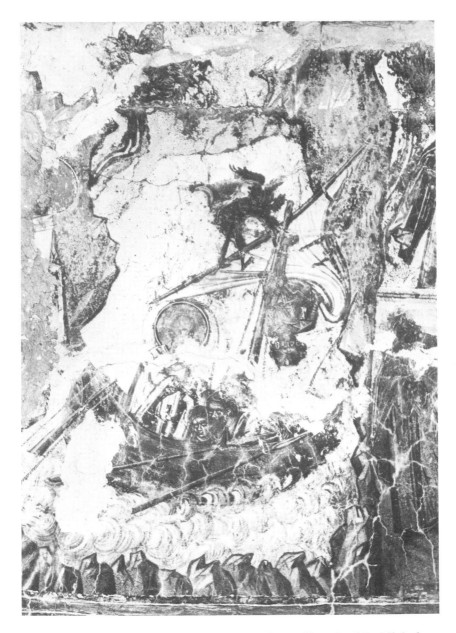

6. Sea scene with devils and Ammonios. Platsa, Church of St. Nicholas
of Kampinari. Mid fourteenth century

7. Sea scene Suceviţa, Church of the Resurrection. Ca. 1600

8. St. Nicholas heals the demoniac brought to the vineyard.
Suceviṭa, Church of the Resurrection. Ca. 1600

9. St. Nicholas is consecrated bishop. Suceviţa, Church of the
Resurrection. Ca. 1600

10. The Death of St. Nicholas. Meteora, Church of St. Nicholas Anapausas.
First half of the sixteenth century

11. The Death of St. Nicholas, detail: singers. Markov Manastir, Church of St. Demetrios. Second half of the fourteenth century

12. The Death of St. Nicholas. Suceviţa, Church of the Resurrection.
Ca. 1600

13. Oblong polykandelon in silver from Holy Sion Monastery. Found at Kumluca, now at Dumbarton Oaks. Mid sixth century

14. Large silver paten with engraved cross from Holy Sion Monastery.
Found at Kumluca, now at Dumbarton Oaks. Mid sixth century

15. Cruciform polykandelon in silver from Holy Sion Monastery. Found at Kumluca, now at Dumbarton Oaks. Mid sixth century

16. Openwork silver container for an oil lamp from Holy Sion Monastery. Found at Kumluca, now at Dumbarton Oaks. Mid sixth century

INDICES

GLOSSARY OF TERMS

Numbers refer to chapter and line in the Greek text. The relevant line in the translation is usually on the level of the Greek line.

archimandrite: **4,** 9; **5,** 3; **13,** 16; **54,** 9; **78,** 25. In the sixth century, a superior of a mandra, "sheepfold," i.e., a monastery, or of monasteries; abbot. In our period, an archimandrite was usually, but not always, a priest.

cubit (πῆχυς): **19,** 5; **24,** 24; **47,** 16. Probably the "woodsawing" or "joiner's" cubit of 1.5 feet = 46.8 cm = ca. 18 3/8 in., rather than the "land-measuring" cubit of 2 feet = 62.46 cm. = ca. 24 5/8 in. Cf. E. Schilbach, *Byzantinische Metrologie* (Munich, 1970), pp. 20-21. If so, the cypress tree of **19** was 1.41 meters = 4 ft. 7½ in. in diameter at the base and 18.80 meters = 61 ft. 4 in. tall; the sickles of the vision in **47** would have been 2.35 meters = 7 ft 8½ in. wide and 7.05 meters = 23 ft. 1½ in. long.

deuterarios: **7,** 15; **12,** 5; **25,** 11, 13; **45,** 3, 13; **46,** 4, 8; **56,** 7; **78,** 18. Second in command in a monastery, assistant to the abbot; prior. The title is well attested in the sixth century.

dismissal: see Liturgy.

Entrance of the Service: see Liturgy.

Formulae:

> *[As] The Lord God lives:* **22,** 9. A biblical formula, cf., e.g., 3 Kings 17.1, 12; 18.10 and Ps 17 (18).46.

> *The Lord hath a long arm:* **26,** 12; **27,** 10; **30,** 7. An unusual formula occuring in our Life only in utterances by Nicholas of Sion.

> *Most beloved of God* (θεοφιλέστατος): **72,** 5; **73,** 7; **75,** 20; **78,** 18; **79,** 6, 8. At the time of our Life, a standard epithet of a bishop (it is only rarely applied to lower ranks, as in the suspect passage **78,** 18, where it is inconsistently used for an archdeacon). The author of our Life combines the epithet with the name of Nicholas of Sion only in passages (**72,** 5; **73,** 7; **75,** 20) that follow upon the story of the latter's elevation to the episcopal dignity (**68**).

One [is] God: **18,** 18. This formula is attested in Jewish writings in Greek, and was frequent in inscriptions coming from the Semitic areas of the Empire. In Christian popular miracle literature, such as the apocryphal Acts of the Apostles and Acts of the Martyrs, it occurs in situations analogous to those of our Life: the apostle or the martyr performs a miracle, and when the gentile crowd or "the people" witness it, they exclaim in wonderment: "One is God." Sometimes that exclamation is followed by a participle (ὁ ἐλεῶν, ὁ σώσας), as in our Life (which has ὁ δώσας). Cf. Erik Peterson, Εἷς Θεός. *Epigraphische, formgeschichtliche und religionsgeschichtliche Untersuchungen* (Göttingen, 1926).

Your Angelic Self: **53,** 12. Literally: "Your angel," i.e., yourself. The same formula is used in the fifth-sixth century Life of Alexander (d. ca. 430), the founder of the monastic rule of the *Akoimetoi.* There it occurs in an address to the bishop of Antioch: "I beseech Your Angel" (τὸν ἄγγελον ὑμῶν) i.e., "I beseech you" (cf. E. De Stoop, ed., *in Patrologia Orientalis*, 6, 5 [1911], p. 689 [= 49, 13-14]). The formula must have become unfamiliar by the eleventh century, for in the Vatican manuscript of our Life it is followed by the words "in front of you" (ἔμπροσθέν σου). We bracketed these words in our Greek text as a later explanatory gloss.

Your Holiness: **8,** 10; **15,** 7; **20,** 8, 23; **26,** 6; **34,** 20; **41,** 8. Polite addresses such as "Your Holiness (ὁσιότης, ἁγιωσύνη)" flourished in late Antiquity and survive in "Your Excellency" today. Two of them occur with some frequency in our Life. On these and similar formulae, cf. A.-J. Festugière, *Vie de Théodore de Sykéôn,* 2 (Brussels, 1970), pp. 187, 191, 228-29.

Indiction: **80,** 3. a) A period of fifteen years used for fiscal purposes and for dating; b) (more frequently) the nth year of a period of fifteen years. This second meaning appears in our passage, where "the thirteenth Indiction" stands for "the thirteenth year of a fifteen year period." Counting by these fifteen-year units started in 312; by the fifth century, the indiction year began on September 1. [Between 541/2 — the beginning of the bubonic plague—and 565— last year of Justinian, under whose rule our Nicholas died, cf. **80,** 4-5—a thirteenth Indiction occured in 549/550 and in 564/565. Only in 564, however, did the tenth of December fall upon a Wednesday (cf. **80,** 3-4). Thus, if the reading "13" of the Vatican manuscript is correct, Nicholas of Sion died in 564.]

Liturgy

dismissal (ἀπόλυσις): **25**, 6. A prayer at the end of a service, dismissing the congregation; end of a service. [The Vatican manuscript, which we follow in our translation, speaks of the "dismissal of the holy assembly," an expression alluding to Acts, 19.40 (41); the Sinai manuscript has "the dismissal of the Divine Liturgy," a more familiar, and therefore probably secondary, formulation.]

Entrance of the Service: **68**, 6. Here, the Little Entrance of the Liturgy of the Catechumens is meant, that is, a procession with the Gospel Book carried through the north door into the church, and back into the altar space through the center, or royal, door. According to some early Ritual books, the ceremony of ordination of a bishop begins when "priests enter to [make] the First Entrance of the Divine Rite; the candidate enters with them, and while the Entrance is being carried out, the Deacon says: 'Wisdom, let us stand straight.' And the candidate, holding the Gospels, enters the altar space." Cf. J. Goar, *Εὐχολόγιον sive Rituale Graecorum* (1730, reprint 1960), p. 252.

reader (ἀναγνώστης): **5**, 7, 12; **61**, 1; **62**, 4, 10; **64**, 3. Holder of the first of the Minor Orders. The reader read the Lessons aloud (at Matins and Vespers) and performed other minor duties, such as lighting the candles.

martyrium: **8**, 9. A Christian building (usually vaulted or domed) going back to the pagan mausoleum or *herôon*. It housed the tomb or relics of a saint (usually, but not always, a martyr), or marked a holy place (site of an holy object or of a Divine manifestation), especially in the Holy Land. Martyria were used for commemorating and celebrating an anniversary of an event, of the saint or of the martyr. Owing to their funerary character, martyria, like cemeteries, were originally located outside the walls of cities, and this may have been the case of the martyrium of Saint Nicholas mentioned in our Life; moreover, at first they were distinct from churches. But by the sixth century martyria begin to be fused with churches, both in function (celebration of a liturgy on an altar over the saint's tomb) and in terms of architecture. The occurrence of the term *martyrion* in our Life does not imply that the Saint Nicholas commemorated there was a martyr.

measure of wine: **55,** 10; **56,** 11. A unit of ca. 10 or 10.25 liters = 2 gallons 2.6 quarts or 2 gallons 2.86 quarts, depending on whether white or red wine was measured. Should the "monastery measure" (seemingly attested for the sixth century) be implied in our text, then the unit value would be 8.2 liters = 2 gallons 0.7 quarts. Cf. E. Schilbach, *Byzantinische Metrologie* (Munich, 1970), pp. 112-13.

modius (μόδιος): **55,** 11 (of bread); **56,** 12 (of grain); **59,** 8 ("large modii" of seed grain); **60,** 4 ("large modii" harvested). A measure of capacity of ca. 17 liters = 4 gallons 2 quarts or 12.8 kg. = 28 lbs. 2½ oz. of wheat. The "large modius" may have been four times larger. If, on the other hand, the "monastic modius" is implied in **55** and **56,** the value of the unit would have been ca. 13.67 liters = 3 gallons 2½ quarts or 10.24 kg. = 22 lbs. 8 oz. of wheat. Cf. E. Schilbach, *Byzantinische Metrologie* (Munich, 1970), pp. 95-96; 98-100. [We should not put too much trust in the numerical values transmitted in manuscripts of our Life, for these values differ from manuscript to manuscript; thus, in **59,** 8, the *Vaticanus* speaks of 25 modii of seed grain, while in the corresponding passage the *Sinaiticus* gives 15 modii.]

nomisma: **56,** 11; **58,** 13; **69,** 19. A gold coin, introduced by Emperor Constantine the Great, of a fineness of 23 to 24 carats and weighing 1/72 of a pound. In the sixth-seventh century a pound (true, calculated on the basis of the weight of contemporary gold coins) amounted to ca. 322 grams; thus on an average, a sixth-century nomisma had a weight of 4.47 grams. The fact that about 600 A.D. a beautiful New Testament on parchment cost three nomismata, a grave digger earned one nomisma per month and at a given moment a bishop had only eight nomismata in his coffers, will give an idea of the coin's purchasing power at this time. Cf., e.g., Philip Grierson, *Catalogue of Byzantine Coins in the Dumbarton Oaks Collection,* 2, 1 (1968), pp. 8-11, and various chapters of John Moschos's *Pratum Spirituale.*

pint (ξέστης): cf. **25,** 10, 16. A liquid measure, probably equal to 0.54 liters, or slightly more than our pint. If so, the three-pint pitcher in **25,** 10, 16 held two modern bottles of wine. Cf. E. Schilbach, *Byzantinische Metrologie* (Munich, 1970), p. 115.

Rossalia: **76,** 1. This word of Latin origin is transmitted in this form only by the Vatican manuscript of our Life (later, it occurs as *rousalia*). It refers to the "feast of the roses," celebrated at the time of the blooming of the roses (in May by the Pagans, around Pentecost by the Christians). Already in pagan times this feast was connected with the cult of the dead; in the Christian period, many a saint was honored at his grave by a *rhodismos,* or a procession combined with the "honoring with roses," celebrated in May, or in the Spring. [As we do not know the duration of the last illness of Nicholas of Sion (he died on December 10), we cannot be quite sure by how long the *Rossalia* of the "forefather" Nicholas preceded our Nicholas's death; in other words, we cannot say for sure whether this feast was celebrated in May (as could be normally expected and as we believe was the case) or whether the celebration took place on December 6, the traditional anniversary of the death of Nicholas of Myra, a mere four days before our Saint's demise. Gustav Anrich proposed the latter date (*Der heilige Nikolaos* . . . , vol. 2, p. 447-449), without considering several common sense objections to his solution. These objections have to do with the need to postulate that our Nicholas's terminal illness lasted but a few days (unless it lasted a whole year and a few days, a duration of which there is no hint in the Life); with the need to assume a considerable speed of travel between Sion and Myra in winter and good passability of roads in the winter season; and with the wisdom of scheduling a Synod in December. To make his hypothesis work, Anrich assumed that the term *Rossalia* was used in our Life in the generic meaning of "festive procession," without reference to the Spring season).]

Sion, Holy; Sion, the holy and glorious one (ἡ ἁγία Σιών· ἡ ἁγία καὶ ἔνδοξος Σιών): for occurrences, *see* General Index. A hill in the southwest of Jerusalem, identified in early centuries with the Old Testament Mount Zion by Christians dwelling there; then, the basilica (built there ca. 400, destroyed in 614) that, according to a tradition going back to the fourth and the late fifth centuries respectively marked the site of the miracle of the Pentecost and of the Last Supper. Also, the name of the monastery of our St. Nicholas in Lycia. Our Life applies to Nicholas's monastery two early formulae that denoted the Christian Sion and its church. The first, "Holy Sion," appears as early as the year 415; the second and longer one, "holy and glorious Sion" (cf. **2,** 3; **4,** 11; **6,** 22; **12, 10; 19,** 16; **80,** 8), occurs in the Liturgy of St. James, the Greek text of which must predate the mid-sixth century. [Does the repeated occurrence of the formula in our Life indicate that the Liturgy of St. James was in use in the Sion monastery?] Cf., e.g., F. Diekamp, *Hippolytos von Theben, Texte und Untersuchungen*

(Münster in Westf., 1898), pp. 96-113; *Reallexikon zur byzantinischen Kunst,* III (1978), 536; 564; 601; P. Maraval, *Lieux saints et pélérinages d' Orient* (Paris, 1985), pp. 257-58; 387.

INDEX OF SCRIPTURAL QUOTATIONS AND ALLUSIONS

Numbers refer to chapter and line of the Greek text.

11, 15 λάμπον — ἥλιος: cf. Mt
17.2

13, 1-2 ἀρχάγγελον τῆς διαθήκης: cf. Mal 3.1

13, 5 δεῦρο, ἀκολούθει μοι: cf.
Mt 19.21; Mk 10.21; Lk
18.22

13, 12-13 δοξάσαι — οὐρανοῖς:
Mt 5.16

13, 13-14 ἐκ κοιλίας γὰρ μητρός: cf., e.g., Jdg 16.17; Ps
21(22).10; 70(71).6; Is 49.1;
Lk 1.15

13, 14 ἐκλελεγμένος: cf. Lk 9.35

14, 1 αὐξηθέντος — παιδίου: cf.
Gen 21.8; Jdg 13.24; Lk
1.80; 2.40

14, 4 σημεῖα. . . .παρέσχεν: cf.
Jn 20.30; *see* also **25, 26.**

17, 9 ἀνέκραγεν — πνεῦμα: cf.
Mk 1. 23; 3.11; Lk 4.33

18, 2 συνάχθητε — 3 ὁμοθυμαδόν: cf. 1 Esd 5.47; 9.38

18, 8 δοῦλε — 9 ἀπολλύμεθα:
cf. Mt 8.25; Mk 4.38; Lk 8.24

18, 17 ἐδόξασαν τὸν θεόν: cf.
Dan 3. 51; Mt 9.8; 15.31; Lk
5.26; 13.13; 23.47; Acts
11.18; 21.20; Gal 1.24

18, 18 ὁ δώσας: — 19 πνευμάτων: cf. Mt 10.1; Mk 6.7

19, 17 ἐδόξαζον — ἐξουσίαν: cf.
Mt 9.8

20, 4 πηγαῖς τῶν ὑδάτων: cf. Ps
17(18).15; 41(42).1; 113(114).
8; Rev 7.17; 8.10; 14.7; 16.4

20, 9 ὁ διάβολος πειράζει: cf.

Mt 4. 1; Mk 1.13; 1 Cor 7.5

20, 11 ἐξῆλθεν — ὑδρεύσασθαι:
cf. Gen 24.43 (v.l.); 1 Kgs 9.11

20, 11 ἀκάθαρτον — 12 ἔρριψεν: cf. Mk 1.26; Lk 4. 35

20, 14 ἀπὸ — ἐκείνης: cf. Mt 9.
22; 15.28; 17.18

20, 27-28: cf. Rom 6.19, 22

20 30-31 πειράζει — διάβολος:
cf. Mt 4.1; Mk 1.13; 1 Cor
7 . 5

21, 3-4 ἀπὸ μικροῦ ἕως μεγάλου: cf. Gen 19.11; 4 Kg 23.
2; 25.26; Jdt 13.4, 13; Is 22.
5, 24; Jer 6.13; 38(31).34; 49
(42).1, 8;51(44).12; Bar 1.4;
1 Macc 5.45; Acts 8.10; Heb
8.11

21, 13 πάντες ὁμοθυμαδόν: cf. 1
Esd 5.58; Jdt 15.5; Acts 5.12

21, 16-17 ἄνθρωπος ἁμαρτωλός: cf. Lk 5.8; Jn 9.16

22, 9 ζῆ κύριος ὁ θεός: cf. 3 Kgs
17.1, 12; 18.10; Ps 17(18).46;
cf. also Am 8.14

22, 13 ἔκραξα δὲ φωνῇ μεγάλῃ:
cf. Mt 27.50; Mk 5.7; Acts
7.57, 60; Rev 6.10

22, 14 φωνή — 15 λέγουσα: cf.
Mt 3.17

22, 19 γίνου — 20 ἄπιστος: cf.
Jn 20.27

23, 10 ἀπὸ μικροῦ ἕως μεγάλου:
cf. Gen 19. 11; 4 Kg 23.2;
25.26; Jdt 13.4, 13; Is 22.5,
24; Jer 6.13; 38 (31).34; 49
(42)1, 8; 51(44).12; Bar 1.4;
1 Macc 5.45; Acts 8.10; Heb
8.11

24, 7 ὁ ζῶν — 8 αἰῶνας: cf. Dan 6.27; 1 Pet 1.23

24, 8 ἐξαπόστειλον — 9 πνεῦμα: cf. Acts 13.26; Gal 4.6

24, 12 ἐν πᾶσι τοῖς ἁγίοις δοξαζεται: cf. Ex 5.11; 1 Pet 4.11

25, 5 τὸ θέλημα τοῦ θεοῦ γενέσθω: cf. Mt 6.10; 26. 42; Lk 22. 42; Acts 21.14

25, 5 ἀπόλυσιν — 6 ἐκκλησίας: cf. Acts 19.40

25, 26 πολλά — ποιεῖ: cf., e,g., Mt 21.15; Jn 11.47; 20.30; Acts 2.43; 5.12; 6.8; 8.6; 14.3; 15.12

26, 4 εἶχεν πνεῦμα ἀκάθαρτον: cf. Mk 3.30; 7.25; Lk 4. 33; Acts 8.7

28, 7-8: cf. Mk 7.25

29, 3 ἐπίφανον — ἡμᾶς: cf. Num 6.25; Ps 66(67).1; 79 (80).3,7,19; 118 (119). 135; Dan 9.17; 3 Macc 6.18

29, 4 ἐπάκουσον — 5 ἐλπιζόντων: cf. Ps 64(65).5; 85(86).1

29, 5 μὴ καταισχύνῃς — 6 ἔλεος: cf. Dan 3.42

29, 5 ποίησον. . . .6 ἐπισκοπήν: cf. Job 29.4; Pr 29.13; Is 23. 17

29, 7 ὅτι ἐπτωχεύσαμεν — 8 οἱ οἰκτιρμοί σου: Ps 78(79).8

30, 1 ἐγένετο — 2 κυμάτων: cf. Mt 8.24

30, 13 κατέπαυσεν — 14 μεγάλη: cf. Mt 8.26; Lk 8.24

31, 11 κάτω — 13 νεκρός: cf. Acts 20.9

31, 16 μὴ κλαίετε — 22 ἡσυχάσατε: cf. Acts 20.10

31, 20 συντετριμμένῳ: cf. Is 61.1; Mt 12.22

31, 28 ἐδόξασαν τὸν θεόν: cf., e.g., Dan 3.51; Mt 9.8; 15.31; Lk 5.26; 13.13; 23.47; Acts 11.18; 21.20; Gal 1.24

32, 12 εἰ θέλημα — ἐστιν: cf., e.g., 1 Th 4.3

32, 18 ἄνθρωπός εἰμι ἁμαρτωλός: cf. Lk 5.8; Jn 9.16

32, 23 ἀνέστησεν — 24 ἐζωοποίησεν: cf., e.g., Jn 5.21; Rom 4.17

32, 24 ἔστη — 25 ὑγιής: cf. Acts 4.10

33, 6 ἰατρούς — 8 τὰ ἐμά: cf. Mk 5.26

33, 13 δύνανται — 15 σπλαγχνισθείς: cf., e.g., Mt 20.34; Mk 1.40-41; 9.22

33, 21 ἠνεῴχθησαν οἱ ὀφθαλμοί: Mt 9.30; Jn 9.10

33, 22 ἐδόξαζεν τὸν θεόν: cf. Dan 3.51; Mt 9.8; 15.31; Lk 5.26; 13.13; 23.47; Acts 11.18; 21.20; Gal 1.24

34, 8 πολλά — 10 πάντα: cf. Mk 5.26

34, 24 ἐξ ὅλης καρδίας: cf. Dt 6.5; Jos 22.5; Mk 12.30,33, Lk 10.27

34, 25 ἀπῆλθεν — 26 δοξάζων τὸν θεόν: cf. Mt 9.7; Lk 5. 24,25; 2 Cor 9.13

35, 13 παρέστη — κυρίου: cf. Acts 27.23; cf. also Lk 1.19; 2 Tim 4.17

37, 1 θελήματι δὲ τοῦ θεοῦ: cf.
Rom 1.10; 1 Pet 4.2
37, 19 λάβωμεν τροφῆς: cf. Acts
2.46; 27.33,34,36
37, 21-22: Ps 54(55).22
37, 28-29 μὴ θλίψῃς ἡμᾶς: cf.
Sir 30.21; 34 (31).31; Mk 3.9

38, 8-9 ἄφες ἐξέλθῃ: cf. Mt 7.4;
27.49
38, 17 τὸ θέλημα — 18 γινέσθω:
cf. Mt 6.10; 26.42; Lk 22.42;
Acts 21.14
38, 20-22: Ps 54 (55).22
38, 23-24 συνήχθησαν ὄχλοι
πολλοί: cf. Mt 13.2; Mk 2.2;
4.1; 5.21

39, 1 ἐν — ἐκείναις: cf. Mt 24.
19, 38; Mk 13.17, 24; Lk 5.35
39, 24 ἐδόξασαν τὸν θεόν: cf.
Dan 3.51; Mt 9.8; 15.31; Lk
5.26; 13.13; 23.47; Acts 11.
18; 21.20; Gal 1.24
39, 26 ὑπακούουσιν αὐτῷ: cf.
Mk 1.27; Heb 5.9

40, 8 ἵνα — 9 ἐφ' ἡμᾶς: cf. Mk
9.22
40, 10 ἐξ — καρδίας: cf. Dt 6.5;
Jos 22.5; Mk 12.30, 33; Lk
10.27

41, 6 ἔρριψαν — 7 πόδας: cf.
Mt 15.30
41, 9 δεινῶς βασανίζει: cf. Mt 8.6
41, 13 ἐξ — καρδίας: cf. Dt 6.5;
Jos 22.5; Mk 12.30, 33; Lk
10.27

42, 2 ἐσπλαγχνίσθη ἐπ' αὐτήν:
cf. Mt 9.36; 14.14; 15.32;
Mk 6.34; 8.2; Lk 7.13.

42, 3 ὁ θεός — 4 γνώστης: Sus
42
42, 4 ὀφθαλμοὺς φωτίζων: cf.
2 Esd 9.8; Ps 12(13).3; 18
(19).8; Sir 31(34).17; Bar
1.12; Eph 1.18
42, 6 λύων — σύνδεσμον: cf. Is
58.6; Dan 5.12
42, 7 παραλελυμένα — διορθωσάμενος: cf. Mt 9.2-8; Mk 2.
1-5; Lk 5.17-26
42, 8 πλήν — ἄλλος cf. 2 Kg
7.22; Wis 12.13; Sir 33(36).5;
Bel 41; cf. also Ex 8.10; Dt
32.39; 1 Kg 2.2; Is 44.6,8;
45.5, 6, 14,21,22
42, 12 ἄνοιξον τὸ στόμα αὐτῆς:
cf., e.g., Ex 4.12,15; Nu 22.
28; Jdg 11.35,36; Job 3.1;
33.2; 35.16; Ps 21 (22).13; 37
(38).13; 38 (39).9; 77(78).2;
108(109).2; 118 (119).13; Pr
24.76,77; 31.27; Wis 10. 21;
Sir 20.15; 22.22; 24.2; 26,
12; 29, 24; 39.5; 51.25; Is
53.7; 57.4; Ezek 3. 27; 33.22;
Dan 10.16; Mt 5.2; 13.35;
Lk 1.64; Acts 8. 35; 10-34;
18.14; 2 Cor 6.11; Rev 13.6
42, 13 μόνον — 14 θεόν: cf. Jn
17.3; 1 Th 1.9; cf. also Is
65.16; Mt 16.16; 26.63; Acts
14.15; 2 Cor 6.16; 1 Tim
3.15; 4.10; Heb 3.12; 9.14;
10.31; 12.22; 1 Pet 1.23; Rev
7.2
42, 16 θελήματι τοῦ θεοῦ: cf.
Rom 1.10; 1 Pet 4.2
42, 16 ὑγιὴς ἐγένετο: cf. Jn 5.9
42, 16 ἀπὸ — 17 ἐκείνης: cf. Mt

Mt 2.10; Mk 16.4; Rev. 16.
21;

53, 17 διάβολος διέσπειρεν: cf.
Mt 13.39

53, 18 πατεῖται: cf. Lk 10.19

54, 5 χαρὰ μεγάλη: cf. Mt 2.10;
28.8; Lk 2. 10

54, 6 δοξάζοντι — 6 αὐτόν:
cf. 1 Kg 2.30

54, 11 ἔφαγον καὶ ἐνεπλήσθησαν: cf. Dt 6.11; 8.12; 11.15;
Neh 9.25; Is 23.18; 44.16; Mt
14.20; Mk 6.42; Lk 9.17; Jn
6.12

54, 11 ἐδοξάσθη ὁ θεός: cf. Jn
7.39; 11.4; 12.16, 23; 13.31,
32; 14.13; 15.8

54, 17 ἀποδώσω — 18 θλίψει
μου: Ps 65 (66).14

55, 11 ἔφαγον — ἐνεπλήσθησαν: cf. Dt 6.11; 8.12; 11.15;
Neh 9.25; Is 23.18; 44.16; Mt
14.20; Mk 6.42; Lk 9.17; Jn
6.12

55, 12-13 ἐδόξασαν τὸν θεόν: cf.
Dan 3.51; Mt 9.8; 15.31; Lk
5.26; 13.13; 23.47; Acts
11.18; 21.20; Gal 1.24

55, 13-14, περιέσσευσεν: Jn
6.13; cf. also Mt 14.20;
15.37; Lk 9. 17; Jn 6.12

56, 15 ἔφαγον καὶ ἐνεπλήσθησαν: cf. Dt 6.11; 8.12; 11.15;
Neh 9.25; Is 23.18; 44.16; Mt
14.20; Mk 6.42; Lk 9.17; Jn
6.12

56, 17, περιέσσευσεν: Jn 6.13;
cf. also Mt 14.20; 15.37; Lk
9. 17; Jn 6.12

56, 21 ἐμπλησθέντες: cf. Dt
6.11; 8.12; 11.15; 31.20

56, 21 ἐδόξασαν — 22 τὸν θεόν:
cf. Dan 3.51; Mt 9.8; 15.31;
Lk 5.26; 13.13; 23.47; Acts
11.18; 21.20; Gal 1.24

56, 26 ἀπὸ μικροῦ ἕως μεγάλου:
cf. Gen 19:11; 4 Kg 23.2; 25.
26; Jdth 13.4, 13; Is 22.5, 24;
Jer 6.13; 38(31).34; 49 (42)1,
8; 51(44). 12; Bar 1.4; 1 Macc
5.45; Acts 8.10; Heb 8.11

56, 26-27 ἐμπλησθέντες: cf. Dt
6.11; 8.12; 11.15; 31.20

56, 27 ἐδόξασαν τὸν θεόν: cf.
Dan 3.51; Mt 9.8; 15.31; Lk
5.26; 13.13; 23.47; Acts 11.
18; 21.20; Gal 1.24

57, 6 ἔφαγον καὶ ἐνεπλήσθησαν: cf Dt 6.11; 8.12; 11.15;
Neh 9.25; Is 23.18; 44.16; Mt
14.20; Mk 6.42; Lk 9.17; Jn
6.12

57, 6-7 ἐδόξασαν τὸν θεόν: cf.
Dan 3.51; Mt 9.8; 15.31; Lk
5.26; 13.13; 23.47; Acts
11.18; 21.20; Gal 1.24

57, 7 περιέσσευσεν: Jn 6.13;
cf. also Mt 14.20; 15.37; Lk
9. 17; Jn 6.12

57, 11 ἐδόξασαν τὸν θεόν: *see*
57, 6-7

57, 17 and 20 ἔδωκαν — θεῷ:
Lk 18.43

57, 23-24 δοξάζων τὸν θεόν: Lk
18.43

57, 27 ἐδόξασαν τὸν θεόν: cf.
Dan 3.51; Mt 9.8; 15.31; Lk
5.26; 13.13; 23.47; Acts
11.18; 21.20; Gal 1.24

65, 9 ἐφυγάδευσεν: cf. Ps 54 (55).8

65, 11 αἰνοῦντα τὸν θεόν: cf. Ps 17(18).3; Lk 2.13,20; Acts 2.47; 3.8,9

66, 4 ἔχων — πονηρόν: cf., e.g., Acts 19.13; cf. also Lk 7.21; 8.2; Acts 19.12,15,16

66, 6-7 ἀπέλυσεν αὐτόν: cf. Mt 18.27; Lk 8.38; 14.4; Acts 4. 21; 17.9

66, 7 ἀπῆλθεν — 8 θεόν: cf. Mt 9.7; Lk 5.24, 25; 2 Cor 9.13

67, 10-11 ἐπιστάσης αὐτῷ ἐπισκιάσεως: cf. Lk 1.35

68, 11-12 ἐδόξασεν αὐτὸν ὁ θεός: cf. 1 Esd 9.52; Sir 3.2

69, 10-11 τοῦ πνεύματος. . . .ἐνδυναμοῦντος: cf. Jdg 6.34 (v.l.); 1 Chr 12.18 (v.l); cf. also 1 Tim 1.12; 2 Tim 4.17

69, 16 εὐχαριστήσας τῷ θεῷ: cf. Lk 18.11; Acts 27.35; 28.15; Rom 1.8; 14.6; 1 Cor 1.4; 14.18; Eph 5.20; Php 1.3, Col 1.3; 3.17; 1 Th 1.2; 2.13; 2 Th 1.3; Rev 11.17

70, 3 ὠχλεῖτο — 4 δαίμονος: cf. Lk 6.18; Acts 5.16

70, 7 ἐνεφύσησεν: Jn 20.22

70, 8-9 ἐδόξασαν . . . . τὸν θεόν: cf. Dan 3.51; Mt 9.8; 15.31; Lk 5.26; 13.13; 23.47; Acts 11.18; 21.20; Gal 1.24

71, 4 ἔρριψεν — ὁσίου: cf. Mt 15.30

71, 6 ἰάθη — 7 ἐκείνης: cf. Mt 9.22; 15.28; 17.18;

71, 7 ἀπῆλθεν — αὐτῆς: cf. Lk 5.24,25

71, 7-8 εὐχαριστοῦσα τῷ Θεῷ: cf. Lk 18.11; Acts 27.35; 28. 15; Rom 1.8; 14.6; 1 Cor 1.4; 14.18; Eph 5.20; Php 1.3; Col 1.3; 3.17; 1 Th 1.2; 2.13; 2 Th 1.3; Rev 11.17

72, 6-7 ὅπως. . .σπλαγχνισθῇ ἐπ᾽ αὐτὸν ὁ θεός: cf. Mt 9.36; 14.14; 15.32; Mk 6.34; 8.2; Lk 7.13

72, 9 ἀπεκατέστη — 11 θεόν: cf. Mt 9.7; 12.13; Lk 5.24,25; Acts 4.10

73, 3 εἶχεν — πονηρόν: cf. Acts 19.13; cf. also Lk 7.21; 8.2; Acts 19.12,15,16

73, 12 ἀπῆλθεν — αὐτοῦ: cf. Lk 5.24,25

73, 13 εὐλογῶν τὸν θεόν: cf. Lk 1.64; 24.53

74, 3 ἔχων — ἀκάθαρτον: cf. Mk 3.30; 7.25; Lk 4.33; Acts 8.7

74, 8 ἀπῆλθεν — αὐτοῦ: cf. Mt 9.7; Lk 5.24, 25

74, 8-9 αἰνῶν τὸν θεόν: cf. Ps 17(18).3; Lk 2.13,20; Acts 2.47; 3.8,9

75, 17 ἀνεχώρησαν εἰς τὰ ἴδια: cf. Acts 21.6; cf. also Jn 1.11; 19.27

75, 22 ἀπέλυσεν αὐτούς: cf. Mt 18.27; Lk 8.38; 14.4; Acts 4.21; 17.9

76, 6 εἰρήνην — 7 ἀποδεδωκός: cf. Jn 14.27; cf. also Lk 12.51; 2 Th 3.16; Heb 12.11

77, 5 παρακαταθήκην: cf. 1 Tim 6.20; 2 Tim 1.12, 14

77, 7-8 εὐχαριστοῦσα τῷ θεῷ: cf. Lk 18.11; Acts 27.35; 28.15; Rom 1.8; 14.6; 1 Cor 1.4; 14.18; Eph 5.20; Php 1. 3; Col 1.3; 3.17; 1 Th 1.2; 2. 13; 2 Th 1.3; Rev 11.17

78, 8 κλίνας τὴν κεφαλήν: Jn 19.30; cf. also Mt 8.20; Lk 9.58

78, 10 ἐπὶ σοί — 12 ἐξελοῦ με: Ps 30 (31).1

78, 13 κύριε — 14 πνεῦμα μου: Ps 30(31).6; cf. also Lk 23. 46

78, 14 μετὰ δόξης: cf. Mt 24.30; Mk 13.26; Lk 21.27; 2 Tim 2.10

78, 14-15 παρέδωκεν τὸ πνεῦ-μα: Jn 19.30

78, 15 εὐλογήσας τὸν θεόν: cf. Lk 1.64; 2.28; 24.53

78, 19, ἀφῆκεν τὴν ψυχήν: cf. Mt 27.50

79, 9-10 καθὼς συνέταξαν: cf. Job 42.9; cf. also Ex 9.12; 12.35; 16.24; 37.20; 38.27; 39.11; Lv 16.34; Nu 8.3, 22; 9.5; 15.36; 17.11; 20.9, 27; 27.11; 31.31, 41; Jos 4.8; 24.30; Jdt 4.8; Dan 15. 41; Mt 21.6; 26.19; 27.10

80, 14 ἐπλήρωσεν τὸν βίον: cf. Acts 13.25

GENERAL INDEX

Entries are quoted by page of the Preface and by chapter and relevant page of the translation.

A

Acts of the Apostles, *see* Scriptures

Agoriane, fresco from, 18

Akalissos, site of the martyrium and monastery of Saint John and dwelling-place of Sabbatios and Nicholas the Elder, **1.**21, **2.**33, [**6**, 27] **11.**31, **13.**35, **54.**87

Akarassos, place-name, **22.**43

Alien, **31.**55, **42.**73; *see* also Devil

Ammonios, a young Egyptian sailor resurrected by Nicholas, 12; **31.**55, **32.**57

Anabos [meaning "slope," "ascent," rather than referring to a place-name Anabos], **18.**39, **75.**107

Andreades, R., 19

Andriake, harbor of Myra, **9.**31; **37.**65; **38.**67

Andronikos, district of, **26.**49

Anrich, G., 17-19

Anthony, blind man at Diolko in Egypt, **33.**59

Apphianos, Saint, shrine at Partaessos, **57.**89

Archangel, shrine at Kroba, **70.**103; at Nea Kome, **56.**89; at Symbolon and Trebendai, **57.**91; at Traglassos [?], **54.**85; *see* also Michael

archimandrite, *see* Glossary of Terms

Arnabanda, village of, **20.**41; **21.**43; **23.**45, **74.**107

Arnabandians, district of, **63.**97

Arneai, place-name, 14; **39.**69; district of, **19.**41; **59.**93

Artemas, brother of Nicholas of Sion and of Hermaios, 5; **7.**29, **39.**69, **44.**75 [**45.**77] **46.**77, [**47.**79], **56.**89; Nicholas' *deuterarios,* **7.**29; [**45.**77] **46.**77, **56.**89, **78.**111 [?]; priest, **7.**29, **78.**111; archimandrite after Nicholas' death, **78.**111

Asia Minor, 11

Askalon, harbor of, **8.**29, **9.**31, **27.**51, **35.**63, **36.**63

B

Bakchos, *see* Sergios

Boyd, S., 19

C

Chatzidakis, M., 19

Chelidon, mountains, **37.**65

Christ, **1.**21, **6.**27, **76.**109; Holy City of (i.e, Jerusalem), **9.**31; minister of (i.e., Nicholas), **47.**79; Kingdom of, **6.**27; *see* also Jesus Christ; Son

Constantine the Great, emperor, 11, 14

Constantinople, **36.**63

Cross, Venerable, *see* Jerusalem

cubits, *see* Glossary of Terms

D

Damasei, hamlet of, **41.**71, **58,**93

151